Index

Chronology

1988–2008

With the end of the war with Russia in sight, Osama and the men around him began to dream of a global Jihad to spread the message of God and to bring the world under Islamic rule. Osama's mentor, Abdullah Azzam, a leading Palestinian Sunni Islamic scholar and theologian, was the first to recognize the necessity for an organized foundation from which believers could launch their struggle for a perfect Islamic world.

But while the orator Azzam talked, the military man acted. Osama called for the first planning meeting that would be named al-Qaeda to be held at his family home in Peshawar, Pakistan. Al- Qaeda was formed in August 1988.

Osama's al-Qaeda organization has both an Islamic arm and a military arm, with the military arm growing in prominence. As new Muslim fighters arrived in Pakistan, they were sent to training camps inside Afghanistan, then dispersed to the various fighting fronts.

As the war with Russia slowed, Osama had more time to devote to the Islamic goals of al-Qaeda. The planning to make Islam the religion of the world increased after he moved from Saudi Arabia to Sudan, and finally to Afghanistan.

December 29, 1992

Aden, Yemen: In an attack targeting American servicemen on their way to Somalia, bombs explode at two hotels in Aden. No soldiers are killed, but two Austrian tourists are.

October 3-4, 1993

Somalia: Somali militia shoot down two American Black Hawk helicopters, killing eighteen U.S. Servicemen.

June 25, 1996:

Dhahran, Saudi Arabia: The Khobar Towers building, a U.S. military housing complex, is bombed, killing nineteen U.S. servicemen.

August 7, 1998:

Kenya and Tanzania: The U.S. embassies of both African nations are car-bombed. More than 222 people are killed, most of them Africans.

October 12, 2000:

Aden, Yemen: Two suicide bombers ram a small boat into the USS Cole while it is docked. The death toll is seventeen American sailors.

September 11, 2001:

Nineteen al-Qaeda suspects hijack four domestic American planes. Two planes are flown into the World Trade Center buildings in New York City. One plane is flown into the Pentagon near Washington, D.C.

The fourth plane crashes into an open field in Pennsylvania when the passengers resist their hijackers. There are various postings of the number of victims, but the most accepted figure seems to be 2,986 innocent people murdered.

February 1, 2002:

Karachi, Pakistan: American journalist Daniel Pearl is kidnapped and beheaded.

April 11, 2002:

Djerba, Tunisia: The Ghriba synagogue is bombed by a natural gas truck. The attack kills fifteen tourists (*fourteen Germans and one Frenchman*) and six Tunisians. Thrirty others are wounded.

October 12, 2002:

Bali, Indonesia: Suicide bombers and car bombs detonate in or near the busy nightclub area, killing over 200 people; 164 tourists and 38 Indonesians. Over 200 others are seriously wounded.

November 28, 2002:

Mombassa, Kenya: A car bomb crashes into the lobby of the Israeli-owned Paradise Hotel and kills sixteen people. During this same time, two surface-to-air missiles are fired at an Israeli charter plane. The missiles miss the plane, saving many lives.

May 12, 2003:

Riyadh, Saudi Arabia: Thirty-four people are killed in a series of bomb attacks targeting housing for foreign nationals and a U.S. office.

May 16, 2003:

Casablanca, Morocco: A series of suicide bombings strike a Spanish restaurant, a hotel, a Jewish center, and the Belgian consulate, killing thirty-three people.

August 5, 2003:

South Jakarta, Indonesia: A car bomb explodes outside the JW Marriott Hotel lobby, killing twelve people and injuring over 150. The dead are four tourists and eight Indonesians.

November 15, 2003, and November 20, 2003:

Istanbul, Turkey: Four car bombs explode at Jewish synagogues, killing fifty-seven and wounding over seven hundred.

2003–2008:

Iraq: There are hundreds of al-Qaeda attacks in every region of Iraq, killing thousands of innocent Iraqis.

March 11, 2004:

Madrid, Spain: Ten bombs explode on commuter trains in Madrid, killing over 190 people and wounding 1,800.

May 29, 2004:

Khobar, Saudi Arabia: Four terrorists attack oil industry installations and the Oasis Compound, a housing compound for foreign workers. The terrorists take fifty foreign nationals hostage, killing twenty-two, some of whom have their throats slit.

June 18, 2004:

Saudi Arabia: American Paul Johnson is kidnapped and held hostage and later beheaded.

July 7, 2005:

London, En gland: Four suicide bombers attack the mass transit system in London, killing fi fty- three and wounding seven hundred.

November 9, 2005:

Amman, Jordan: Simultaneous bombings in three different American-franchise hotels kill fi fty-seven people and injure 120 others.

April 11, 2007:

Algiers: Two bombs explode, one at a police station and the other at the offi ce of the Algerian prime minister, killing thirty- three people.

June 2, 2008:

Pakistan: The Danish embassy is struck by a car bomb, killing six people and injuring many others.

Bin Laden's Family

According to repors prepared by Soufan Group, Osama's mother, Allia, was born in 1943 in Latakia, Syria. After marriage to Mohammed bin Laden in 1956, she moved to Saudi Arabia, where their only child, Osama, was born in Riyadh on February 15, 1957. When Osama was only a year old, Allia became pregnant a second time, but lost the child after a freak accident when she was injured by a faulty wringer- washer machine.

Shortly after the miscarriage, Allia asked her husband for a divorce, which was granted. Living in a world where divorced women cannot live alone, Allia married for a second time, to Muhammad al-Attas, a kindly man an respected employee of her former husband's rapidly expanding construction company.

Allia and Muhammad al-Attas became the parents of four children, three sons and a daughter. Osama lived with his mother, stepfather, and four siblings in the Mushraf neighborhood of Jeddah, where he grew up, and where he brought his first cousin and first bride, Najwa.

Mohammed Bin Laden

Although there are no official birth records, it is believed that Osama bin Laden's father was born between 1906 and 1908 in Rubat, Hadramaut, located in southeastern Yemen. After Mohammed's father died unexpectedly, he traveled with his younger brother, Abdullah, to seek employment outside Yemen.

After a series of misadventures, the two brothers settled in Saudi Arabia, where Mohammed won the trust of the first king of Saudi Arabia, Abdul Aziz al-Saud, for his work on various construction projects. With the backing of the king, Mohammed soon formed the Saudi bin Laden Group, which grew to be one of the largest companies in Saudi Arabia. Later the company spread into other countries in the region.

The increasingly prosperous Mohammed bin Laden married many women and became the father of numerous children, twenty-two sons and thirty-three daughters.

Wives

Najwa Ghanem, married in 1974

Najwa Ghanem was born in 1958 in Latakia, Syria, to Ibrahim and Nabeeha. Ibrahim married five times before marrying Nabeeha. He had only one son from his previous marriages, a boy named Ali. Nabeeha was his sixth and final wife. Ibrahim and Nabeeha were the parents of five children, born in this order: Naji, Najwa, Nabeel, Ahmed, and Leila. Najwa married her seventeen-year-old cousin Osama in 1974 when she was fifteen.

After four or five months, Osama, Allia and Muhammad al-Attas traveled to Syria to escort Najwa to her new home in Jeddah, Saudi Arabia. Ibrahim went with his daughter and remained in Jeddah for a visit.

Najwa and Osama became the parents of eleven children. Najwa moved with her husband from Saudi Arabia to Sudan, and then to Afghanistan. Between September 7 and 9, 2001, Najwa left Afghanistan for good. She now lives with her family in Syria. Her son Abdul Rahman and her two youngest daughters live with her.

Khadijah sharif, married in 1983

Nine years older than her ex-husband, Osama, Khadijah is from a family descended from the Prophet. A highly educated woman, she had worked as a teacher before marrying Osama bin Laden. After giving birth to three children, and while living in Sudan, she divorced her husband and returned to live in Saudi Arabia where she still lives. Her eldest son, Ali, is in prison in Saudi Arabia, having been sentenced to fifteen years for allegedly possessing an illegal weapon.

Khairiah Sabar, married in 1985

Khairiah's family is also descended from the Prophet. Educated to teach deafmute children, Khairiah became Osama's third wife after Najwa arranged the marriage. The mother of one son, Hamza, Khairiah remained in Afghanistan with her husband after the events of September 11, 2001.

Siham Sabar, married in 1987

Siham's family is also descended from the Prophet. She is Osama's fourth wife and the mother of four children. She remained in Afghanistan with her husband and children after the events of September 11, 2001.

Amal

Dismissing the marriage that was annulled, Amal is Osama's fifth wife and bore him one daughter, named Safia.

Children with First Wife, Najwa Ghanem

Najwa's first child and eldest son, Abdullah, was born in Jeddah in 1976. As the eldest son, Abdullah held the most honored position of all the children of Osama bin Laden. When he became a teenager, Abdullah began to speak his opinion on matters affecting the family.

Abdullah left the family in Khartoum in 1995 when he traveled to Jeddah, Saudi Arabia, to marry his cousin, Tiayba Mohammed bin Laden. Abdullah chose not to return to Khartoum, instead remaining in Jeddah with his wife and children where he operates a small business. Abdullah lives a quiet life, shunning all publicity, although he remains close to his mother, Najwa, whom he visits in Syria.

Najwa's second child and second son, Abdul Rahman, was born in Jeddah in 1978. Abdul Rahman was an exceptional child who had to face unique personal trials. Abdul Rahman departed Afghanistan with his mother in September 2001. Since that time, Abdul Rahman has been unable to reinstate his Saudi nationality and has found it diffcult to find employment or to marry without official papers. A talented horse man, Abdul Rahman lives quietly with his mother and two youngest siblings in Latakia, shunning all publicity like his elder brother.

Najwa's third child and third son was born in Jeddah in 1979. A garrulous child, Sa'ad remained overly talkative even as an adult, often exasperating his brothers and other acquaintances. Osama refused permission for Sa'ad, his Sudanese-born wife, or their son, Osama, to leave Afghanistan with Najwa.

Najwa's fourth child and fourth son was born in Jeddah in 1981. Omar was the son closest to his mother and the son who most vigorously rebelled against his father and his Jihad. In fact, it has been Omar's dream to counter his father's violent Jihad by organizing a peace movement that will find a better way to solve cultural and religious differences.

After leaving Afghanistan for the final time in 2001, Omar has met many challenges. Although successful in having his Saudi citizenship restored, it has been difficult for Omar to find his place in the business world. Omar married and had one son, Ahmed.

When traveling in Egypt, Omar met an Englishwoman, Jane Felix-Browne. The couple fell in love, bringing his first marriage to an end. Since that time, Omar has become even more passionate in calling for an end to violence, longing for the bin Laden name to become linked with peace rather than with terrorism.

Wishing to join his wife to live in the United Kingdom, where he believes he will find it easier to form a peace movement, Omar applied for a routine marriage visa. Problems arose, with his visa application determined quest for politic asylum. Finally, through the generosity of the government of Qatar, Omar and his wife settled there while waiting for his visa.

Najwa's fifth child and fifth son was born in 1983 in Jeddah, Saudi Arabia. In 2001 Osman married the daughter of Egyptian Mohammed Shawky al-Islambouli, a high-ranking member of Sheikh Omar Abdel Rahman's al-Gama'a'al-Islamiyya group and who was closely affiliated with Osama Bin Laden's al-Qaeda group.

Osman's father-in-law, along with 107 other defendants, had previously been indicted in 1997 by the Egyptian government in the conspiracy to assassinate President Hosni Mubarak of Egypt, as well as other Egyptian leaders. Al-Islambouli's brother, Khalid, was infamous for being the lead assassin of President Sadat on October 6, 1981.

Khalid had shouted, "Death to Pharaoh" as he ran towards Sadat to shoot him. Khalid was arrested and at trial found guilty of the crime and executed the following year, in April 1982.

Osama would not allow Osman or his wife to depart Afghanistan with Najwa. Rumors have circulated that Osman escaped Afghanistan during the October/November 2001 bombings by the American government, along with Dr. Ayman al- Zawahiri, but there is no firm evidence of this. Najwa does not know the fate of her fifth born son or his wife.

Najwa's sixth child and sixth son was born in 1985 in Jeddah. Mohammed was his father's second choice for his successor as head of al-Qaeda. Up until he expressed his disapproval of violence, Omar had been his father's first choice.

Omar also says that of all his brothers, Mohammed is the only brother possessing some of the qualities necessary to assume an important position in his father's organization. After marrying the daughter of Abu Hafs in 2000,

Najwa's seventh child and first daughter was born in Medina in 1987. After Omar suggested a groom, Osama then arranged for the marriage of Fatima to a Saudi fighter named Mohammed in 1999 when Fatima was twelve years old. Her husband was killed in the American attacks of October and November 2001.

Najwa's eighth child and second daughter was born in Jeddah in 1990. Iman was only eleven years old when her mother left Afghanistan on September 9, 2001. Osama refused Najwa's request that her young daughter leave with her.

Najwa's ninth child and seventh son was born in 1993 in Jeddah when Najwa left Khartoum to fly to Saudi Arabia especially for his birth. Ladin was only seven years old when Najwa left Afghanistan on September 9, 2001.

Najwa's tenth child and third daughter, Rukhaiya was born in Jalalabad, Afghanistan, in 1997. Because of her extreme youth, Osama allowed Najwa to take Rukhaiya with her to Syria in 1999 when she left to give birth to her eleventh child. Najwa was also allowed to take Rukhaiya with her when she left Afghanistan for the final time on September 9, 2001. Rukhaiya is living with her mother in Syria.

Najwa's eleventh child and fourth daughter was born in Latakia, Syria, in 1999. Osama had granted Najwa's request to take Nour, along with her sister Rukhaiya and one brother, Abdul Rahman, when she left Afghanistan in September 2001. Nour is living with her mother in Syria.

Children with Second's Wife, Khadijah

Khadijah's first child and first son with Osama was born in Jeddah, Saudi Arabia. After Khadijah and Osama divorced, Khadijah left Khartoum and returned to live in Saudi Arabia. Ten-year-old Ali accompanied his mother to Saudi Arabia, but returned the following year for one visit to Khartoum to see his father and half-siblings. A few years ago, Ali was arrested by Saudi security and charged with the illegal possession of a weapon.

Khadijah's second child and second son with Osama was born in Jeddah in 1990. When Khadijah left Khartoum to return to Saudi Arabia, Amer went with his mother, never seeing his father again. Today Amer is living in Saudi Arabia.

Khadijah's third child and first and only daughter with Osama was born in Khartoum, Sudan, in 1992. In 1993, when Khadijah left Khartoum to return to Saudi Arabia, Aisha went with her mother, never seeing her father again. Today Aisha is living in Saudi Arabia.

Child with third Wife, Khairiah

Khairiah's first child and first son with Osama was born in 1989 in Jeddah, Saudi Arabia. As of 2001, Hamza was Khairiah's only child.

Children with fourth Wife, Siham

Siham's first child and first daughter with Osama was born in 1988 in Jeddah, Saudi Arabia. At her 1999 wedding arranged by her father, Kadhija was married to a Saudi al-Qaeda fighter named Abdullah in 1999, when she was only eleven years old. Kadhija remained in Afghanistan with her mother and she was there during the American bombings of October and November 2001.

Siham's second child and first son with Osama, Khalid, was born in 1989 in Jeddah, Saudi Arabia. Little is known about Khalid, although he remained with his mother in Afghanistan. He was kilied in Abbottabad in May 2011 during the raid of US Navy Seal's Team Six against the compound of Osama Bin Laden.

Siham's third child and second daughter with Osama was born in 1990 in Jeddah, Saudi Arabia. Born prematurely, and on the same day as Najwa's daughter Iman, Miriam had a challenging early life. Little is known of Miriam other than she remained with her mother in Afghanistan.

Child with Fifth Wife Yemeni Amal al- Sadah

Amal's first child and first daughter with Osama. Although Safia's mother married Osama bin Laden in Kandahar, Afghanistan, prior to Najwa's leaving the country, unlike his other marriages, Najwa knew little of Amal. Today there is no firm information about Amal al- Sadah or her daughter, Safia. Some reports have Osama sending Amal and Safia back to Yemen and out of danger before the September 11, 2001, attacks on the United States, while others say that Amal and Safia remained with Osama and his extended family, fleeing Afghanistan into Pakistan.

Hamza Bin Laden

According to Ali Soufan's article published in CTC Sentinel in September 2017, «Hamza bin Ladin was among his father's favorite sons, and he has always been among the most consistently fervent of his siblings in his support for violent jihad. Now in his late 20s, Hamza is being prepared for a leadership role in the organization his father founded. As a member of the bin Ladin dynasty, Hamza is likely to be perceived favorably by the jihadi rank-and-file.

With the Islamic State's 'caliphate' apparently on the verge of collapse, Hamza is now the figure best placed to reunify the global jihadi movement. Hamza bin Ladin's mother, Khairia Sabar, is a child psychologist from the respected al-Hindi family of Saudi Arabia. The pair had been introduced when Saad, one of bin Ladin's sons by his first wife, Najwa al-Ghanem, had attended Khairia's clinic to receive therapy for a mental disorder. Khairia was single, in her mid-30s, and in fragile health—an unpropitious situation for a woman in a conservative kingdom where teenage brides are far from uncommon.

Bin Ladin, by contrast, was seven years younger, the son of a billionaire, and already making a name for himself as a fundraiser for the mujahideen struggle against the Soviets in Afghanistan. Moreover, by this time, bin Ladin already had two wives. But Najwa, the first of them, encouraged him to pursue Khairia, believing that having someone with her training permanently on hand would help her son Saad and his brothers and sisters, some of whom also suffered from developmental disorders.

Not surprisingly given Khairia's age and state of health, she and bin Ladin struggled to conceive. Over the first three years of their marriage, as bin Ladin moved back and forth between Saudi Arabia and the theater of war in Afghanistan, she endured miscarriage after miscarriage. During this time, bin Ladin added a fourth wife to the family—another highly educated Saudi woman, Siham Sabar.

Then, in 1989, both Siham and Khairia bore him sons. Siham's was called Khalid, a name that in Arabic means "eternal." Khairia's boy was named Hamza, meaning "steadfast." Thenceforward, in accordance with ancient Arab custom, Khairia became known by the honorific Umm Hamza, the Mother of Hamza. The boy would remain her only child by bin Ladin, but that fact has by no means diminished either Hamza's importance or Khairia's.

In 1991, reeling from a series of bloody embarrassments in Afghanistan and dismayed by the Saudi government's increasing hostility toward him, bin Ladin moved al-Qa`ida's base of operations to Sudan, just across the Red Sea from his home city of Jeddah.

Among bin Ladin's inner circle of top lieutenants and their families, Umm Hamza soon developed a reputation for level-headedness and wise counsel. As bin Ladin's longtime bodyguard Abu Jandal put it, she was "respected by absolutely everyone." In Sudan, Khairia set up an informal school to teach the wives and children of al-Qa`ida members about Islamic theology, gave advice on religious matters, and from time to time even offered marriage counseling.

At a time when al-Qa`ida could easily have disintegrated under the weight of its forced exile and bin Ladin's growing fear of arrest or assassination, Khairia's calm and optimistic influence played an important role in holding the organization together

Hamza was seven years old when the regime of Omar Bashir finally caved to international pressure and expelled al-Qa`ida from Sudan. Bin Ladin and his entourage decamped to Afghanistan, where they were offered safe haven first by local warlords and subsequently by the Taliban movement, which overran most of the country within a few months of bin Ladin's arrival.

Al-Qa`ida's new hosts gave bin Ladin the choice of several desirable residences, including a former royal palace. Characteristically, however, he *chose instead a base in the mountains near Jalalabad consisting of concrete huts lacking power, water, and in many cases even doors.*

Bin Ladin eventually moved to Tarnak Farms, a camp complex outside Kandahar with almost as little in the way of creature comforts. Not everyone relishes this kind of austerity; while bin Ladin was still in Sudan, his second wife, Khadija Sharif, had divorced him, citing the hardships of life in a militant camp. His first wife, Najwa, would finally leave him on the eve of 9/11. But Khairia and Siham—the mothers of Hamza and Khalid, respectively—were ready to go through significant privations for their husband, and both would be with him at the very end.

In Afghanistan, Hamza emerged as one of bin Ladin's favorite sons. Still not yet a teenager, he appeared in propaganda videos alongside his father, underwent assault training with al-Qa`ida fighters, and preached fiery sermons in a young boy's helium voice. In December 2000, aged 11, Hamza was chosen to recite a poem at the wedding of his 15-year-old brother, Mohammed. His assured performance transfixed the other guests; bin Ladin family members would talk about it, and even have dreams about it, for years to come.

But already, Hamza's time with his father was drawing to a close. On September 10, 2001, anticipating the backlash that would follow his latest and most outrageous assault on the United States, bin Ladin ordered his wives and their younger children out of his Kandahar compound—a conspicuous target and one that had been bombed before—to seek shelter in Jalalabad, 350 miles northeast.

There, al-Qa`ida's propagandists shot one last video featuring Hamza, in which the boy can be seen reciting a poem praising the bravery of Kabul's Taliban defenders and handling wreckage claimed to be from a downed U.S. Helicopter.

The video was, of course, a travesty. The Taliban, far from mounting a stalwart defense, were already being routed up and down the country, and the helicopter wreck, certainly not American, was most likely that of a Soviet gunship shot down before Hamza was born, probably with surface-to-air missiles supplied by the United States.

As bin Ladin made ready to ride south for his last stand at Tora Bora, he ordered his family east, over the border into Pakistan. This decision made sense. Al-Qa`ida had found shelter there during and immediately after the war against the Soviets, and operatives like Khalid Sheikh Mohammed had long lived with impunity in Pakistani megacities like Karachi.

But 9/11 had changed this picture along with everything else. General Pervez Musharraf responded to the attacks by turning Pakistan into an enthusiastic supporter of the United States' efforts against al-Qa`ida and the Taliban. Faced with a rapidly narrowing range of risky options, al-Qa`ida decided that its people, including bin Ladin's family, should leave Pakistan and seek refuge in the neighboring country of Iran.

The world's foremost Shi`a stronghold may seem an odd destination for an organization populated by Sunni extremists, men who pepper their public utterances with slurs against Shi`a Muslims, calling them "rejectionists" and "apostates." But in the fall of 2001, with support for the United States at an all-time high, Iran suddenly became the one place in the Muslim world where America's writ could be counted upon not to run.

Inside Iran, Saif al-`Adl, a wily Egyptian ex-soldier who had been a pivotal figure in al-Qa`ida since its inception, oversaw a secret network of safe houses. In the beginning, it seemed as if al-Qa`ida had found at least temporary sanctuary. But Hamza nevertheless chafed against the constraints of this life in the shadows.

In July 2002, he wrote a poem to his father, bemoaning the "spheres of danger everywhere I look" and asking, "What has happened for us to be chased by danger?"

In his response, bin Ladin did not sugar-coat matters for his 12-year-old son. "I can see only a very steep path ahead," he wrote. "A decade has gone by in vagrancy and travel, and here we are in our tragedy… for how long will real men be in short supply?"

Further hardship lurked just over the horizon. For if Hamza and his family thought they had evaded detection, they were wrong. In fact, it seems that Iranian intelligence knew of al-Qa`ida's presence on the Islamic Republic's soil right from the start. Around April 2003, the al-Qa`ida members in Iran realized they were being watched and began to take steps to thwart Tehran's monitoring.

Fearing that al-Qa`ida might slip through their fingers, the authorities initiated a dragnet that pulled in practically every al-Qa`ida operative and family member in the country.

For the next few years, Hamza and his mother were held at a succession of military facilities in the Tehran area, some cramped and dingy, others spacious and relatively comfortable, but always separated from the outside world by high walls, razor wire, and surveillance cameras. Despite their tribulations, Khairia remained adamant that her son should receive the best *possible education under the circumstances.*

Her own pedagogic efforts continued, and to supplement these, she solicited a group of bin Ladin's top lieutenants being held in the same facility, including al-`Adl, to educate Hamza in Qur'anic study, Islamic jurisprudence, and the hadith (alleged deeds and sayings of the prophet). Hamza is said to have become learned in each of these subjects.

Hamza matured in other ways, too. While still in captivity, he married the daughter of one of his teachers, the longtime al-Qa`i-da military commander Abu Mohammed al-Masri. Hamza's new wife soon gave birth to a son and a daughter, whom they named respectively Usama and Khairia. Hamza told the elder bin Ladin that "God created [my children] to serve you." And he longed to rejoin his father. "How many times, from the depths of my heart, I wished to be beside you," Hamza wrote in 2009. "I remember every smile that you smiled at me, every word that you spoke to me, every look that you gave me."

Neither captivity nor fatherhood could dim the desire to follow in his father's footsteps, which Hamza had shown from a precociously early age. On the contrary, as time went on, he grew ever more desperate to reenter the fray. His greatest frustration, he told his father in a letter smuggled out to Abbottabad, was that "the mujahidin legions have marched and I have not joined them." But bin Ladin was determined to ensure a different destiny for his favorite son.

Iran's double game

With so many senior al-Qa`ida members in custody, Iran possessed huge leverage over bin Ladin's organization. By 2010, however, al-Qa`ida had acquired a bargaining chip of its own in the shape of a captive Iranian diplomat sold to them as a hostage by Pakistani tribal elements.

With the Haqqani Network acting as go-between, a prisoner swap was arranged. In August 2010, at the beginning of Ramadan, Hamza was released along with his mother, wife, and children. Two of his older brothers, Uthman and Mohammed, soon followed along with their own families.

All those released made their way to Waziristan, where a sizable al-Qa`ida contingent lived under the protection of various Pakistani militant groups. The bin Ladin family was spread across several countries. Abdullah, Usama's eldest son, was living a "quiet life" as a businessman in Saudi Arabia.

Another son, Ladin, previously imprisoned in Iran, had gone to stay with his grandmother's side of family in Syria. Another, Omar, lived in Qatar for a time before moving to Saudi Arabia. Bin Ladin therefore had a number of possible places to send family members freed from Iran. He wanted his sons Uthman and Mohammed to stay in Pakistan, provided a "safe place" could be found for them.

His initial plan on hearing of Hamza's release was to try to have him sent to Qatar. Given that Hamza had been imprisoned in Iran from around the age of 14, it would be "difficult [for the United States or other countries] to indict him and to ask Qatar to extradite him." Moreover, in Qatar, the home of Al-Jazeera, Hamza would enjoy relative freedom of speech, which he could exploit in order to act as a spokesperson for bin Ladin's brand of Islam, to "spread the jihadi doctrine and refute the wrong and the suspicions raised around jihad."

But Mahmud, bin Ladin's Libyan chief of staff—also known as Atiyya Abdul Rahman—balked at the idea of Qatar as a destination, on the basis that the small Gulf state, a U.S. ally, would hand Hamza over to the Americans.

Ultimately, as will be seen, bin Ladin followed Mahmud's advice; but the suggestion that Hamza should act as a mouthpiece for jihadi dogma indicates that, despite their long separation, the father had more than an inkling of his son's rhetorical abilities.

In Abbottabad, five hundred miles northeast of al-Qa`ida's Waziristan powerbase, bin Ladin already had one grown son with him—Khalid, the son of his fourth wife, Siham, born in the same year as Hamza. Khalid served as the compound's resident handy-man and plumber.

He also kept a cow he had bought from a local farmer and, like all of the men around bin Ladin, was prepared to defend his father with deadly force. Khalid was useful to have around, to be sure, but hardly suited for leadership. Now, however, three more adult sons hid in Waziristan, awaiting their father's call: Uthman, aged 27, Mohammed, 25, and Hamza, just 21.

Bin Ladin made his choice. He ordered Uthman and Mohammed to go to Peshawar, 100 miles from their father. Khalid was to do the same, having been betrothed to a girl whose family lived there. But Hamza was to come to Abbottabad as soon as he could safely do so. As Khairia told him in a letter, "The father ... asks God that he will benefit from you ... He has prepared a lot of work for you."

For a while, the portents seemed encouraging. Siham, Khalid's mother, told Hamza of a "very good" dream in which "you were conducting Adhan [the

Muslim call to prayer] from a top a very high building, in the same voice in which you said, 'Stay strong my father, for heaven awaits us and victory is ours if God permits.'" This was a reference to the poem that Hamza had recited at his brother Mohammed's wedding more than a decade previously.

As ever, security was the overriding factor, and bin Ladin had already lost one son in Waziristan. Saad, a decade older than Hamza, had been imprisoned in Iran alongside his brothers, but by mid-August 2008, he had been set free or had escaped, depending on which account one believes.

Like Hamza, he made his way to Waziristan. Saad, characteristically, grew restless, perhaps as a result of the mental problems treated by Khairia back in Jeddah. Whatever the cause, Saad apparently behaved recklessly, showed his face once too often in public, and sometimes in the first half of 2009, was killed by a U.S. missile. Mahmud, bin Ladin's chief of staff, told his commander in a letter that "Saad died—peace be upon him—because he was impatient."

"We pray to God to have mercy on Saad," bin Ladin wrote. "And may He reward us with a substitute." For Hamza, Mahmud had nothing but praise. "He is very sweet and good," he told bin Ladin. "I see in him wisdom and politeness. He does not want to be treated with favoritism because he is the son of 'someone.'"

Eager as he was for Hamza to join him, bin Ladin was not going to allow the younger son to meet the same fate as the elder. He therefore issued operatives in Waziristan with strict instructions to keep Hamza indoors unless absolutely necessary and insisted on personally vetting the man assigned to guard his son. Under these strictures, which Mahmud likened to a "prison," Hamza—usually as patient and level-headed as his mother—began to exhibit some of Saad's petulance. Bin Ladin relented a little, allowing Hamza to undergo shooting practice.

Bin Ladin agonized over the decision to bring his son to his side. On the one hand, Hamza was the heir presumptive—the son of his favorite wife, charismatic and well-liked. He could be a great help to the organization. On the other hand, bin Ladin's own security situation, already precarious to begin with, had recently become yet more delicate, for the two Pakistani brothers who protected him and his family were dangerously close to burning out from stress.

One of them, Ahmed, had contracted a serious illness that bin Ladin feared might relapse at any time.They could hold out, bin Ladin estimated, at most another few months. Bin Ladin needed to find replacements for the brothers as soon as possible, but his requirements were exacting. In order to blend in, the new protectors would need to be Pakistanis, fluent in local dialects. To avoid raising suspicions about the unusual size of the compound, they would need to have large families. And, of course, they would need to be absolutely trustworthy and relentlessly committed to the cause.

Mahmud would have his work cut out fulfilling such a tall order. In the meantime, however, bin Ladin finally decided, despite the obvious danger, to have Hamza join him. By early April 2011, Mahmud had hatched a plan to make it happen. Hamza, with his wife and children, traveled south, through the badlands of Baluchistan.

This was a roundabout route, to be sure, but it was safer than heading directly toward Abbottabad over the Khyber mountain passes. Once in Baluchistan, the plan was for Hamza's party to rendezvous with Azmarai, one of al-Qa`ida's most seasoned and trusted fixers. Azmarai would arrange forward passage through Karachi and then by air or train to Peshawar.

There, Hamza would meet another al-Qa`ida operative who would send him on to Abbottabad when the time was right. To ease his brother through the inevitable check-points along the way, Khalid lent Hamza his fake ID and driver's license. By late April 2011, plans were afoot, and Hamza waited only for a cloudy sky to speed him on his way. But it was not to be. Within a few weeks, his father was dead.

Hamza may have avoided death or capture in Abbottabad by weeks or even days. His brother Khalid was not so lucky; he died wielding an assault weapon in a futile attempt to defend his father against the superior numbers, tactics, and technology of the U.S. Navy SEALs.

Hamza's mother, Khairia, was taken into Pakistani custody in the early hours of May 2, 2011. Around a year later, she, Umm Khalid, and a dozen other bin Ladin family members were deported to Saudi Arabia, where they live to this day in a compound outside Jeddah under what their lawyer describes as "very tight restrictions and security arrangements made by the Kingdom's authorities," including a ban on speaking publicly about their time in Pakistan.

Islamic State during Hamza's mature

The Islamic State takes pride in claiming the Jordanian terrorist, Abu Musab al Zarqawi (*Ahmad Fadeel al Nazal al Khalayleh*) as its founder and inspiration, and it has been assiduously polishing his reputation through its online propaganda.

Zarqawi

On a cold and blustery evening in December 1989, Huthaifa Azzam, the teenage son of the legendary Jordanian-Palestinian mujahideen leader Sheikh Abdullah Azzam, went to the airport in Peshawar, Pakistan, to welcome a group of young men. All were new recruits, largely from Jordan, and they had come to fight in a fratricidal civil war in neighboring Afghanistan —an outgrowth of the CIA-financed jihad of the 1980s against the Soviet occupation there.

The men were scruffy, Huthaifa mused as he greeted them, and seemed hardly in battle-ready form. Some had just been released from prison; others were professors and sheikhs. None of them would prove worth remembering —except for a relatively short, squat man named Ahmad Fadhil Nazzal al-Khalaylah. He would later rename himself Abu Musab al-Zarqawi.

Once one of the most wanted men in the world, for whose arrest the United States offered a $25 million reward, al-Zarqawi was a notoriously enigmatic figure—a man who was everywhere yet nowhere.

Huthaifa Azzam bridges both worlds. He first went into battle at the age of fifteen, fighting against the Soviets in Afghanistan with his father and Osama bin Laden (to whom his father was a spiritual mentor); three years later, on that December night at the Peshawar airport, he met al-Zarqawi for the first time.

The two Azzams and bin Laden had fought against the Soviets in the early days of the jihad; al-Zarqawi would fight in the war's second phase, after the Soviets had pulled out. Both Huthaifa Azzam and al-Zarqawi would eventually leave Afghanistan to pursue two very different lives, but their paths would once again cross on the battlefields of jihad in Iraq, after the U.S. invasion of 2003.

A self-described jihadist—one who believes in struggle, or, more loosely, holy war—Azzam now lives in the Jordanian capital, Amman, where he is at work on a doctorate in classical Arabic literature, but he moves routinely between Jordan and Iraq.

Abu Musab al-Zarqawi, barely forty and barely literate, a Bedouin from the Bani Hassan tribe, was until recently almost unknown outside his native Jordan. Then, on February 5, 2003, Secretary of State Colin Powell catapulted him onto the world stage. In his address to the United Nations making the case for war in Iraq, Powell identified al-Zarqawi—mistakenly, as it turned out—as the crucial link between al-Qaeda and Saddam Hussein's regime. Subsequently, al-Zarqawi became a leading figure in the insurgency in Iraq—and in November of last year, he also brought his jihadist revolution back home, as the architect of three lethal hotel bombings in Amman.

His notoriety grew with every atrocity he perpetrated, yet Western and Middle Eastern intelligence officials remained bedeviled by a simple question: Who was he? Was he al-Qaeda's point man in Iraq, as the Bush administration argued repeatedly? Or was he, as a retired Israeli intelligence official told not long ago, a staunch rival of bin Laden's, whose importance the United States exaggerated in order to validate a link between al-Qaeda and pre-war Iraq, and to put a non-Iraqi face on a complex insurgency?

Bin Laden and Zarqawi had little in common: bin Laden, like most of his inner circle, is a university graduate from an influential family; al-Zarqawi, like many who follow him, was from an anonymous family (even though they are members of a significant tribe) and an anonymous town—a man who was fired from a job as a video-store clerk and whose background included street gangs and, according to Jordanian intelligence officials, prison for sexual assault.

He was a ruthless self-promoter who, U.S. officials claim, killed or wounded thousands of people in three years (2003-2006)—in suicide bombings, mass executions, and beheadings that have been videotaped. He developed a mythic aura of invulnerability. But he was not the terrorist mastermind that he was often claimed to be.

Zarqa is a shambolic industrial city of some 850,000 people, a sprawl of factories, open fields, and dust. Twenty-five miles northeast of Amman, it is Jordan's third-largest city, and one of its most militant. For years it has been a magnet for Islamic activists. Along with the cities of Irbid and Salt, it has sent the largest number of Jordanian volunteers to fight abroad, first in Afghanistan and now in Iraq.

Al-Zarqawi was born and raised in the al-Masoum neighborhood of Zarqa's old city, which sprawls somewhat haphazardly into the al-Ruseifah Palestinian refugee camp. (*More than 60 percent of Jordan's 5.9 million inhabitants are Palestinian, as are some 80 percent of the inhabitants of old Zarqa.*)

Until his death, al-Zarqawi kept a home on a quiet lane in Zarqa. It was indistinguishable from its neighbors—a two-story white stucco building surrounded by a whitewashed wall. The house was empty,; al-Zarqawi's sisters, who still live in Zarqa, would come by to look after it.

The first of al-Zarqawi's two wives had lived in the house until recently. She was his cousin, whom he had married when he was twenty-two. They had four children, two boys and two girls. But not long before my visit, al-Zarqawi had sent an unknown man to drive them across the border to be with him in Iraq.

His second wife, a Jordanian-Palestinian whom he had married in Afghanistan, and with whom he has a son, was reported to be with him in Iraq as well. Al-Zarqawi's mother, Omm Sayel, whom he adored—and who had traveled to Peshawar with him when he joined the jihad—died of leukemia in 2004; although he was the most wanted man in Jordan at the time of her death, al-Zarqawi returned to Zarqa in disguise to attend her funeral.

Afganistan

Al-Zarqawi was based initially in the border town of Khost, which, after both the Americans and the Soviets had left Afghanistan, was the site of intense and heavily contested battles between the mujahideen and the pro-Soviet Najibullah regime. At the beginning, al-Zarqawi had not been a fighter but had tried his hand at being a journalist. He had worked as a reporter for a small jihadist magazine, *Al-Bonian al Marsous*.

"He was an ordinary guy, an ordinary fighter, and didn't really distinguish himself," Huthaifa Azzam said of al-Zarqawi's first time in Afghanistan. *"He was a quiet guy who didn't talk much. But he was brave. Zarqawi doesn't know the meaning of fear. He's been wounded five or six times in Afghanistan and Iraq. He seems to intentionally place himself in the middle of the most dangerous situations. He fought in the battles of Khost and Kardez and, in April 1992, witnessed the liberation of Kabul by the mujahideen.*

A lot of Arabs were great commanders during those years. Zarqawi was not. He also wasn't very religious during that time. In fact, he'd only 'returned' to Islam three months before coming to Afghanistan. It was the Tablighi Jamaat [a proselytizing missionary group spread across the Muslim world] who convinced him—he had thirty-seven criminal cases against him by then—that it was time to cleanse himself."

His second time in Afghanistan was far more important than the first. But the first was significant in two ways. Zarqawi was young and impressionable; he'd never been out of Jordan before, and now, for the first time, he was interacting with doctrinaire Islamists from across the Muslim world, most of them brought to Afghanistan by the CIA.

It was also his first exposure to al-Qaeda. He didn't meet bin Laden, of course, but he trained in one of his and Abdullah Azzam's camps: the Sada camp near the Afghan border inside Pakistan. He trained under Abu Hafs al-Masri." (*The reference was to the nom de guerre of Mohammed Atef, an Egyptian who was bin Laden's military chief and, until he was killed in an American air strike in Afghanistan in November 2001, the No. 3 official in al-Qaeda.*)

Abu Muntassir Bilah Muhammad is another jihadist who spent time fighting in Afghanistan and who would later become one of the co-founders of al-Zarqawi's first militant Islamist group. "*Zarqawi arrived in Afghanistan as a zero, a man with no career, just floundering about. He trained and fought and he came back to Jordan with ambitions and dreams: to carry the ideology of jihad. His first ambition was to reform Jordan, to set up an Islamist state. And there was a cachet involved in fighting in the jihad. Zarqawi returned to Jordan with newfound respect. It's not so much what Zarqawi did in the jihad —it's what the jihad did for him.*"

With an eye to the future, al-Zarqawi also used the jihad years to begin the process of cultivating friendships that would eventually lead to the formation of an international support network for his activities. Particularly when he was in Khost, his primary friendships were with the Saudi fighters and others from the Gulf. Some of them were millionaires. There were even a couple of billionaires.

But perhaps as important as anything else, it was in Afghanistan that al-Zarqawi was introduced to Sheikh Abu Muhammad al-Maqdisi (*whose real name is Isam Muhammad Tahir al-Barqawi*), a revered and militant Salafist cleric who had moved to Zarqa following the mass expulsion of Palestinians from Kuwait in the aftermath of the Gulf War.

The Salafiya movement originated in Egypt, at the end of the nineteenth century, as a modernist Sunni reform movement, the aim of which was to let the Muslim world rise to the challenges posed by Western science and political thought. But since the 1920s, it has evolved into a severely puritanical school of absolutist thought that is markedly anti-Western and based on a literal interpretation of the Koran.

Today's most radical Salafists regard any departure from their own rigid principles of Islam to be heretical; their particular hatred of Shiites—who broke with the Sunnis in 632 A.D. over the question of succession to the Prophet Muhammad, and who now constitute the majority in Iran and Iraq—is visceral. Over the years, al-Maqdisi embraced the most extreme school of Salafism, closely akin to the puritanical Wahhabism of Saudi Arabia, and in the early 1980s he published *The Creed of Abraham*, the single most important source of teachings for Salafist movements around the world.

Al-Zarqawi and al-Maqdisi left Afghanistan in 1993 and returned to Jordan. They found it much changed. In their absence the Jordanians and the Israelis had begun negotiations that would lead to the signing of a peace treaty in 1994; the Palestinians had signed the Oslo Accords of 1993; and the Iraqis had lost the Gulf War. Unemployment was up sharply, the result of a privatization drive agreed to with the International Monetary Fund, and Jordanians were frustrated and angry.

The Muslim Brotherhood—the kingdom's only viable opposition political force, which had agreed to support King Hussein in exchange for being allowed to participate in public and parliamentary life—appeared unable to cope with the rising disaffection. Small underground Islamist groups had therefore begun to appear, composed largely of men who had fought in the Afghan jihad, and who were guided by the increasingly loud voices of militant clerics who felt the Muslim Brotherhood had been co-opted by the state.

After the two men returned home, al-Maqdisi toured the kingdom, preaching and recruiting, and al-Zarqawi sought out Abu Muntassir, who had already acquired a standing among Islamic militants in Jordan. Despite their enthusiasm, al-Zarqawi, al-Maqdisi, and Abu Muntassir did not appear to be natural revolutionaries.

Their first operation was in Zarqa, in 1993, when al-Zarqawi dispatched one of their men to a local cinema with orders to blow it up because it was showing pornographic films. But the hapless would-be bomber apparently got so distracted by what was happening on the screen that he forgot about his bomb. It exploded and blew off his legs.

In another botched operation, al-Maqdisi (according to court testimony that he denied) gave al-Zarqawi seven grenades he had smuggled into Jordan, and al-Zarqawi hid them in the cellar of his family's home. Al-Maqdisi was already under surveillance by Jordan's intelligence service by that time, because of his growing popularity.

The grenades were quickly discovered, and the two men, along with a number of their followers, found themselves for the first time before a state security court. Al-Zarqawi told the court that he had found the grenades while walking down the street. The judges were not amused. They convicted him and al-Maqdisi of possessing illegal weapons and belonging to a banned organization. In 1994, al-Zarqawi was sentenced to fifteen years in prison. He would flourish there.

Al-Zarqawi embraced prison life in the extreme—as he appears to have embraced everything. According to fellow inmates of his, his primary obsessions were recruiting other prisoners to his cause, building his body, and, under the tutelage of al-Maqdisi, memorizing the 6,236 verses of the Koran. He was stern, tough, and unrelenting on anything that he considered to be an infraction of his rules, yet he was often seen in the prison courtyard crying as he read the Koran.

He was fastidious about his appearance in prison—his beard and moustache were always cosmetically groomed—and he wore only Afghan dress: the *shalwar kameez* and a rolled-brim, woolen Pashtun cap. Islamists flocked to him. He attracted recruits; some joined him out of fascination, others out of curiosity, and still others out of fear. In a short time, he had organized prison life at Swaqa like a gang leader.

There were also confrontations and altercations with prison officials and guards. Whether al-Zarqawi was ever tortured is a matter of dispute: some of his followers say he was; Jordanian government officials, perhaps predictably, say he was not.

Al-Zarqawi controlled not only his followers but also the ward's television sets. No one could really *watch* them, however, since he had covered them with black cloth to prevent the display of female forms. All the inmates could do was listen—and only to the evening news at eight o'clock.

Al-Zarqawi and al-Maqdisi's Bayat al-Imam continued to grow, both inside prison and in Zarqa, Irbid, and Salt. Al-Zarqawi used his Bedouin credentials to good effect, as his own profile began to ascend. His Bani Hassan tribe is one of the Middle East's most prominent, and its tribal lands spill across the borders dividing Jordan, Syria, and Iraq.

In Jordan, many of its members hold high-level positions in the government, the army, and the intelligence service. As a result, many of the prisoners, and many of Swaqa's guards, deferred to al-Zarqawi. Al-Maqdisi, a Palestinian, was also accorded special treatment, but largely as a result of his links to al-Zarqawi and the Bani Hassan. Between mentor and pupil, the roles had subtly begun to shift inside the prison walls.

As al-Zarqawi recruited, al-Maqdisi preached, and using the Internet, they broadcast their message of jihad across three continents. Sheikh Abu Qatada, a Palestinian cleric who is one of Salafism's leading ideologues, was also one of al-Maqdisi's closest friends. The two men had been together in Kuwait, then in Zarqa, then Afghanistan. Abu Qatada, after leaving Afghanistan, had moved to London (where he is currently under arrest, awaiting possible deportation to Jordan).

Now al-Maqdisi's religious tracts were smuggled out of Swaqa by prisoners' wives and mothers, with help from sympathetic prison guards, and they were sent on to Abu Qatada, who posted them on the Web sites of Salafists and jihadists throughout Europe, the Middle East, and the Persian Gulf.

Al-Zarqawi's own religious views became increasingly severe, as did his intolerance of anyone he believed to be an infidel. Al-Maqdisi sometimes angrily disagreed with him. It was the first portent of what lay ahead. Al-Zarqawi began to eclipse his mentor in prison, and would continue to do so over the coming years, but their final, and public, break did not occur until November 2005, when, on Al-Jazeera, al-Maqdisi criticized his former protégé for the hotel bombings in Amman. Nevertheless, despite their prison disagreements, al-Maqdisi, from time to time, permitted al-Zarqawi to draft his own religious tracts. Abu Muntassir who would also later break with al-Zarqawi was his editor.

In May of the following year (1999), Jordan's King Abdullah II—newly enthroned after the death of his father, King Hussein—declared a general amnesty, and al-Zarqawi was released from Swaqa. He had made effective use of his time there. As he had done nearly a decade before—when he befriended wealthy Saudi jihadists in Khost—he had expanded his reach and his appeal during his prison years. Among the fellow inmates he had converted to Salafism and brought into the Bayat al-Imam were a substantial number of prisoners from Iraq.

After returning for a few months to Zarqa, al-Zarqawi left again and traveled to Pakistan. He may or may not have known that Jordan was about to declare him a suspect in a series of foiled terrorist attacks intended for New Year's Eve of 1999. The plan, which became known as the "Millennium Plot," involved the bombing of Christian landmarks and other tourist sites, along with the Radisson Hotel in Amman. Had it succeeded, it would have been al-Zarqawi's first involvement in a major terrorist attack.

Whatever the case, al-Zarqawi planned ahead before he left for Pakistan. He arrived bearing a letter of introduction from Abu Kutaiba al-Urduni, one of Jordan's most significant leaders during the jihad in Afghanistan. Al-Urduni had been a key deputy to—and the chief recruiter inside Jordan for—Sheikh Abdullah Azzam, Huthaifa Azzam's father. Having worked for years in Peshawar as the leader of the Service Office, or the Maktab al-Khidmat, the sheikh had become *the* pivotal figure in the Pan-Islamic recruitment of volunteers for the jihad.) Al-Urduni's letter was the first endorsement that al-Zarqawi had received from such a senior figure—and the letter was addressed to Osama bin Laden.

In December 1999, al-Zarqawi crossed the border into Afghanistan, and later that month he and bin Laden met at the Government Guest House in the southern city of Kandahar, the de facto capital of the ruling Taliban. According to several different accounts of the meeting, bin Laden distrusted and disliked al-Zarqawi immediately. He suspected that the group of Jordanian prisoners with whom al-Zarqawi had been granted amnesty earlier in the year had been infiltrated by Jordanian intelligence.

Something similar had occurred not long before with a Jordanian jihadist cell that had come to Afghanistan. Bin Laden also disliked al-Zarqawi's swagger and the green tattoos on his left hand, which he reportedly considered un-Islamic. Al-Zarqawi came across to bin Laden as aggressively ambitious, abrasive, and overbearing. His hatred of Shiites also seemed to bin Laden to be potentially divisive—which, of course, it was. Bin Laden's mother, to whom he remains close, is a Shiite, from the Alawites of Syria.

Al-Zarqawi would not recant, even in the presence of the legendary head of al-Qaeda. "Shiites should be executed," he reportedly declared. He also took exception to bin Laden's providing Arab fighters to the Taliban, the fundamentalist student militia that, although now in power, was still battling the Northern Alliance, which controlled some 10 percent of Afghanistan. Muslim killing Muslim was un-Islamic, al-Zarqawi is reported to have said. Unaccustomed to such direct criticism, the leader of al-Qaeda was aghast.

A former Egyptian army colonel who had trained in special operations, al-Adel was then al-Qaeda's chief of security and a prominent voice in an emerging debate gripping the militant Islamist world. Who should the primary target be —the "near enemy" (the Muslim world's "un-Islamic" regimes) or the "far enemy" (primarily Israel and the United States)?

Al-Zarqawi was a near-enemy advocate, and although his obsession remained the overthrow of the Jordanian monarchy, he had expanded his horizons slightly during his prison years and had now begun to focus on the area known as al-Sham, or the Levant, which includes Jordan, Syria, Lebanon, and historic Palestine.

As an Egyptian who had attempted to overthrow his own country's army-backed regime, al-Adel saw merit in al-Zarqawi's views. Thus, after a good deal of debate within al-Qaeda, it was agreed that al-Zarqawi would be given $5,000 or so in "seed money" to set up his own training camp outside the western Afghan city of Herat, near the Iranian border. It was about as far away as he could be from bin Laden. Saif al-Adel was designated the middleman.

In early 2000, with a dozen or so followers who had arrived from Peshawar and Amman, al-Zarqawi set out for the western desert encircling Herat. His goal: to build an army that he could export to anywhere in the world. Al-Adel paid monthly visits to al-Zarqawi's training camp; later, on his Web site, he would write that he was amazed at what he saw there.

The number of al-Zarqawi's fighters multiplied from dozens to hundreds during the following year, and by the time the forces evacuated their camp, prior to the U.S. air strikes of October 200l, the fighters and their families numbered some 2,000 to 3,000. According to al-Adel, the wives of al-Zarqawi's followers served lavish Levantine cuisine in the camp.

It was in Herat that al-Zarqawi formed the militant organization Jund al-Sham, or Soldiers of the Levant. His key operational lieutenants were mainly Syrians —most of whom had fought in the Afghan jihad, and many of whom belonged to their country's banned Muslim Brotherhood. The Brotherhood's exiled leadership, which is largely based in Europe, was immensely important in recruiting for the Herat camp, although whether it also supplied funds remains under debate. What is clear, however, is that al-Zarqawi's closest aide, a Syrian from the city of Hama named Sulayman Khalid Darwish—or Abu al-Ghadiyah—was considered to be, one of al-Zarqawi's most likely successors.

For Zarqawi, it was the turning point. Herat was the beginning of what he is now. He had command responsibilities for the first time; he had a battle plan. And even though he and bin Laden never got on, he was important to them. Herat was the only training camp in Afghanistan that was actively recruiting volunteers specifically from the Sham. In Herat, he called himself the 'Emir of Sham'!"

At least five times, in 2000 and 2001, bin Laden called al-Zarqawi to come to Kandahar and pay *bayat*—take an oath of allegiance—to him. Each time, al-Zarqawi refused. Under no circumstances did he want to become involved in the battle between the Northern Alliance and the Taliban. He also did not believe that either bin Laden or the Taliban was serious enough about jihad.

When the United States launched its air war inside Afghanistan, on October 7, 2001, al-Zarqawi joined forces with al-Qaeda and the Taliban for the first time. He and his Jund al-Sham fought in and around Herat and Kandahar. Al-Zarqawi was wounded in an American air strike—not in the leg, as U.S. officials claimed for two years, but in the chest, when the ceiling of the building in which he was operating collapsed on him. Neither did he join Osama bin Laden in the eastern mountains of Tora Bora, as U.S. officials have also said. Bin Laden took only his most trusted fighters to Tora Bora, and al-Zarqawi was not one of them.

In December 2001, accompanied by some 300 fighters from Jund al-Sham, al-Zarqawi left Afghanistan once again, and entered Iran. During the next fourteen months, al-Zarqawi based himself primarily in Iran and in the autonomous area of Kurdistan, in northern Iraq, traveling from time to time to Syria and to the Ayn al-Hilwah Palestinian refugee camp in the south of Lebanon—a camp that became his main recruiting ground.

More often, however, al-Zarqawi traveled to the Sunni Triangle of Iraq. He expanded his network, recruited and trained new fighters, and set up bases, safe houses, and military training camps. In Iran, he was reunited with Saif al-Adel—who encouraged him to go to Iraq and provided contacts there—and for a time, al-Zarqawi stayed at a farm belonging to the fiercely anti-American Afghan jihad leader Gulbaddin Hekmatyar. In Kurdistan he lived and worked with the separatist militant Islamist group Ansar al-Islam, ironically in an area protected as part of the "no-fly" zone imposed on Saddam Hussein by Washington.

One can only imagine how astonished al-Zarqawi must have been when Colin Powell named him as the crucial link between al-Qaeda and Saddam Hussein's regime. He was not even officially a part of al-Qaeda, and ever since he had left Afghanistan, his links had been not to Iraq but to Iran.

In the beginning the Iranians gave him automatic weapons, uniforms, military equipment, when he was with the army of Ansar al-Islam. Now they essentially just turn a blind eye to his activities, and to those of al-Qaeda generally. The Iranians see Iraq as a fight against the Americans, and overall, they'll get rid of Zarqawi and all of his people once the Americans are out.

In the summer of 2003, three months after the American invasion, al-Zarqawi moved to the Sunni areas of Iraq. He became infamous almost at once. On August 7, he allegedly carried out a car-bomb attack at the Jordanian embassy in Baghdad. Twelve days later, he was linked to the bombing of the United Nations headquarters, in which twenty-two people died.

And on August 29, in what was then the deadliest attack of the war, he engineered the killing of over a hundred people, including a revered cleric, the Ayatollah Muhammad Baqr al-Hakim, in a car bombing outside Shia Islam's holy shrine in Najaf. The suicide bomber in that attack was Yassin Jarad, from Zarqa. He was al-Zarqawi's father-in-law.

Even then—and even more so now—Zarqawi was not the main force in the insurgency. To establish himself, he carried out the Muhammad Hakim operation, and the attack against the UN. Both of them gained a lot of support for him—with the tribes, with Saddam's army and other remnants of his regime. They made Zarqawi the *symbol* of the resistance in Iraq, but not the leader. And he never has been."

The Americans have been patently stupid in all of this. They've blown Zarqawi so out of proportion that, of course, his prestige has grown. And as a result, sleeper cells from all over Europe are coming to join him now.

Of course, no one did more to cultivate that image than al-Zarqawi himself. He committed some of the deadliest attacks in Iraq, though they still represent only some 10 percent of the country's total number of attacks. In May 2004, he inaugurated his notorious wave of hostage beheadings; he also specialized in suicide and truck bombings of Shiite shrines and mosques, largely in Shiite neighborhoods.

His primary aim was to provoke a civil war. "*If we succeed in dragging [the Shia] into a sectarian war,*" he purportedly wrote in a letter intercepted by U.S. forces and released in February 2004, "*this will awaken the sleepy Sunnis who are fearful of destruction and death at the hands of the Shia.*"

Al-Zarqawi courted chaos so that Iraq would provide him another failed state to operate in after the overthrow of the Taliban in Afghanistan. He became best known for his videotaped beheadings. One after the other they appeared on jihadist Web sites, always the same. In the background was the trademark black banner of al-Zarqawi's newest group: al-Tawhid wa al-Jihad, or Monotheism and Jihad. In the foreground, a blindfolded hostage, kneeling and pleading for his life, was dressed in an orange jumpsuit resembling those worn by the detainees at Guantánamo Bay.

Al-Zarqawi's first victim was a Pennsylvania engineer named Nicholas Berg. In the video, five hooded men, dressed in black, stand behind Berg. After a recitation, one of the men pulls a long knife from his shirt, steps forward, and slices off Berg's head. The U.S. military quickly announced that the executioner was al-Zarqawi himself, and although no one doubts that he planned the operation, questions soon arose: the figure seems taller than al-Zarqawi, and he uses his right hand to wield the knife. Al-Zarqawi was said to be left-handed.

Regardless of his growing notoriety in Iraq, al-Zarqawi never lost sight of his ultimate goal: the overthrow of the Jordanian monarchy. His efforts to foment unrest in Jordan included the 2002 assassination of the U.S. diplomat Lawrence Foley, and, on a far larger scale, a disrupted plot in 2004 to bomb the headquarters of the Jordanian intelligence services—a scheme that, according to Jordanian officials, would have entailed the use of trucks packed with enough chemicals and explosives to kill some 80,000 people. Once it was uncovered, al-Zarqawi immediately accepted responsibility for the plot, although he denied that chemical weapons would have been involved.

Later that year, in October 2004, after resisting for nearly five years, al-Zarqawi finally paid *bayat* to Osama bin Laden—but only after eight months of often stormy negotiations. After doing so he proclaimed himself to be the "Emir of al-Qaeda's Operations in the Land of Mesopotamia," a title that subordinated him to bin Laden but at the same time placed him firmly on the global stage.

One explanation for this coming together of these two former antagonists was simple: al-Zarqawi profited from the al-Qaeda franchise, and bin Laden needed a presence in Iraq. Another explanation is more complex: bin Laden laid claim to al-Zarqawi in the hopes of forestalling his emergence as the single most important terrorist figure in the world, and al-Zarqawi accepted bin Laden's endorsement to augment his credibility and to strengthen his grip on the Iraqi tribes. Both explanations are true. It was a pragmatic alliance, but tenuous from the start.

The attacks, which represented an expansion of al- Zarqawi's sophistication and reach, also showed his growing independence from the al-Qaeda chief. They came only thirteen months after he had sworn *bayat*. The alliance had already begun to fray.

The signs were visible as early as the summer of 2005. In a letter purportedly sent to al-Zarqawi in July from Ayman al-Zawahiri, the Egyptian surgeon who is bin Laden's designated heir, al-Zarqawi was chided about his tactics in Iraq. And although some experts have cast doubt on the letter's authenticity (it was released by the office of the U.S. Director of National Intelligence), few would dispute its message: namely, that al-Zarqawi's hostage beheadings, his mass slaughter of Shiites, and his assaults on their mosques were all having a negative effect on Muslim opinion—both of him and, by extension, of al-Qaeda—around the world. In one admonition, al-Zawahiri allegedly advised al-Zarqawi that a captive can be killed as easily by a bullet as by a knife.

Then, in early April, Huthaifa Azzam announced that the "Iraqi resistance's high command" had stripped al-Zarqawi of his political role and relegated him to military operations. It was the second time that al-Zarqawi's profile had seemingly been lowered—or that he had lowered it—this year. The first had come in January, when it was announced that al-Qaeda in Iraq had joined five other Sunni insurgent groups to form a coalition called the Mujahideen Shura Council. By early May, U.S. counterterrorism analysts were still puzzling over what the two events meant and what changes they could portend.

As they debated, al-Zarqawi sprang to life again, in a video posted on the Internet on April 24. It was the first time he had appeared in a jihadist videotape, and the first time he had shown his face. Dressed in black fatigues and a black cap, he had ammunition pouches strapped across his chest. He appeared fit, if overweight, as he posed in the desert firing an automatic weapon and as he sat with a group of masked aides, apparently plotting strategy.

It seemed an extremely risky thing for him to do, and yet it also appeared to be very deliberate. It was a useful tool for recruitment, intending to show al-Zarqawi as both a flamboyant fighter and a pensive strategist. More important than anything else, however, it was meant to show the world that Abu Musab al-Zarqawi—the brash young man who had come of age in the rough-and-tumble of Zarqa—remained relevant.

Al Maqdisi

It is news to few observers that thousands, even millions, of young Muslims are influenced—to some extent—by jihadi literature circulating on various Islamist websites and discussion forums. The mujahideen's use of the internet for communication, indoctrination, recruitment and public relations has been well demonstrated.

Through this medium, a field of preachers and ideologues compete for the vast audience of young Muslims, attempting to sway their opinion and bring them to the "correct" practice and understanding of Islam. Those backing the global jihadi movement have succeeded in capturing this audience—perhaps more so than other contenders—and have gained a wide following of careful but loyal readers.

The literature is critical because it provides deeper motivation to the believer, who seeks ideological backing before taking action. A group of Muslim scholars—*Abu Muhammad al-Maqdisi, Abu Basir al-Tartusi, Abu Qatada al-Filistini, 'Abd al-Qadir bin 'Abd al-'Aziz* and a few other Saudi clerics—are the primary Salafi opinion-makers guiding the jihadi movement. These scholars are relied upon for their credibility since they have either been imprisoned or exiled by their home countries. They are also perceived as being true to Islam and putting the interests of Muslims before themselves, making them sincere, legitimate and incorruptible. For the mujahideen, they are portrayed as scholarly authorities and the source for doctrinal legitimacy.

Surprisingly, al-Qaeda leaders Osama bin Laden and Ayman al-Zawahiri are not highly cited in jihadi literature. They are not considered authorities in Islamic law or looked to as the ideological force behind the jihadi movement. Indeed, in the world of Salafi-Jihadi ideology, they are relatively minor players. One possible reason for this is that the two are figureheads, pioneers in carrying out successful attacks against one of the enemies of Muslims.

This suggests that there is a role for charismatic leaders to bring Muslims to jihad, as soldiers to the battlefield, but there is a separate role for these Salafi scholars in setting the broader goals for the movement, the limits and terms of engagement and selecting valid and legal targets. They are, in essence, creating the Islamic legal framework for this struggle so that the basis upon which it is waged will be sound. It is then left to strategists and mujahid leaders to conduct successful campaigns within this framework.

There is no single governing body for determining Islamic law in the Muslim world. Movements tend to center around persuasive and influential scholars that can grant them legitimacy in the eyes of other Muslims. This has been the case for the Salafi movement, including militant Salafis who form the global jihadi movement.

Although the mujahideen are not held accountable to their constituency, they understand the need for their fellow Muslims to support their actions, provide them with funding and safe haven and ultimately be able to mobilize them when needed. Accordingly, the advice and writings of Salafi scholars carry much weight with the mujahideen and Muslim readers—regardless of their affiliation.

For the most influential scholars of the Salafi movement, such as Abu Muhammad al-Maqdisi, Abu Qatada and Abu Basir, the end goal is never jihad itself. The objective is to bring Muslims to a Salafi reading of Islam and then to deliver salvation to the global Muslim community. As such, the primary element of the literature is the meaning and implementation of the Sharia.

The scholars first bring their interpretation of Islamic law on various political and social issues and present their advice on the appropriate action. The common ground among the scholars behind the jihadi movement is their rejection of Muslims living under apostate laws and political systems governing outside what God has decreed. The required response—for all, but to differing degrees and with differing tactics—is resistance.

This drive to instill Islamic law into Muslim society, and ultimately recreate that society under their interpretation of the law, often translates into an endorsement for violent jihad as practiced by bin Laden and others. While there are many Muslim scholars who call for these sources of law to be the primary factors in how Muslims live, the important distinction lies in how one should confront political systems that rule by law other than Sharia.

The debate over law and society is critical in jihadi literature. It establishes the framework through which young Muslims should struggle; for these scholars, it is clear their aim is not jihad, but the creation of such a society through jihad, an obligatory struggle for the believer.

Biography

Asim Tahir al-Barqawi, better known as Abu Muhammad al-Maqdisi, is one of the most prolific contemporary jihadi ideologues and a classically trained scholar. He was born in Nablus in 1959, but has been imprisoned intermittently since the 1990s by the Jordanian authorities for his criticism of the government and calls for jihad.

Al-Maqdisi is regarded as one of the highest living authorities in Islam for Salafis, jihadis and other conservative Sunni Muslims who share elements of his program. His imprisonment, however, seems to have had little effect on his scholarly output. He was the most frequently cited living Salafi scholar, indicating the wide range of jihadis (*from strategists to mujahideen to fellow scholars*) that cite his writings.

Al-Maqdisi is well traveled; he moved to Kuwait as a child and later undertook studies in the University of Mosul in Iraq. After that al-Maqdisi traveled through Saudi Arabia, Pakistan and Afghanistan, where he met various jihadi groups and wrote some of his most famous books, such as *Millat 'Ibrahim wa da'awet al-anbiya wa'l murseleen* (The Creed of Abraham and the Preaching of the Prophets and the Deliverers) and *Al-kawashif al-jaliyya fi kufr al-dawla al-Sa`udiyya* (The Shameful Actions Manifest in the Saudi State's Disbelief).

In 1992 al-Maqdisi returned to Jordan and started to preach his ideology, which quickly spread among some youngsters. The shaykh criticized Jordanian officials, denouncing their rule as illegitimate and opposed to the Shari`a. A combination of direct rhetoric and well-circulated stories of how he confronted the judges and his interrogators by calling them tyrants and disbelievers, soon established al-Maqdisi as a charismatic ideologue and leader of Salafi-Jiahdism.

Al-Maqdisi's texts are frequently aimed at the youth in Jordanian prisons and similar Muslims around the world that are encouraged to hold steadfast to the path of jihad in accordance with the principles of Islamic law detailed in his texts. To be sure, the legal arguments are lost on many of his students who lack formal Islamic legal training, but he provides contemporary examples to buttress his points.

Many of his texts are in response to criticisms of jihad by other Salafi clerics, typically from the Gulf states or Saudi Arabia. Other writings include the education of the next generation of leaders, numerous issues relating to resistance to tyrannical regimes and the need to uphold the Sharia and one of his most-widely read works, the Creed of Abraham, on monotheistic faiths (*which is highly critical of contemporary Christians and Jews*).

Through his writings, al-Maqdisi sets out the "correct" agenda for the various mujahideen groups to follow, what their intentions and objectives should be as they enter jihad, what preparation is required and what they should avoid (*such as hasty actions that make the mujahideen look inept, inexperienced, or indifferent to killing innocent Muslims*).

There are more nuanced discussions of espionage, defining apostasy, takfir (*labeling another Muslim an unbeliever*), different examples of interaction with tyrannical rule and explanations of when resistance is obligatory for the believer. Yet, in the end, a clear direction is set out for the mujahideen and those who support their cause on how best to proceed.

Al-Maqdisi's calls for unity are respected because of the scholarly weight behind his name and reputation. This also exposes one of the movement's weaknesses, and the shortcomings of governments confronting jihadi ideologues: a blow to his standing or a publicly lost debate would likely do much more to damage the unity of the jihadi movement than would his imprisonment.

On March 12, 2008 Abu Muhammad al-Maqdisi—born Isam Muhammad Tahir al-Barqawi in 1959—was released from a Jordanian prison after almost three years imprisonment without trial. Maqdisi has long played a pivotal role in defining jihadist ideology. After taking part in the Afghan jihad of the 1980s, he refined the ideology of declaring takfir against other Muslims—i.e. defining them as apostates and thus deserving of death—leading to the creation of jihadist groups in Jordan and 1995 attacks in Saudi Arabia—whose government he had denounced as un-Islamic as early as 1989.

Between 1995 and 1999, Maqdisi was imprisoned in Jordan, during which time he expanded his ideas and built new radical networks with the help of his right-hand man, Abu Musab al-Zarqawi. From 1999, Maqdisi has spent most of his time in Jordanian prisons, reemerging briefly in 2005 before being re-imprisoned for giving an interview to al-Jazeera television in which he criticized Zarqawi's attacks on civilians while reiterating his support for a broader jihad against the West and "un-Islamic" governments. Despite his long prison terms, however, Maqdisi has written and distributed several accessible books addressing key issues such as democracy, takfir and jihadist tactics, giving him an almost unmatched influence over the evolution of jihadist theory.

Maqdisi's Influence

Maqdisi's latest release from prison—apparently on grounds of ill-health—was reported extensively on radical Islamic websites. Significantly, even Islamic extremists outside the Arab world reacted euphorically to the news of his release. For example, a senior member of *the islamicawakening.com* forum, a prominent English-language Salafi website, responded to news of his release by writing: "AllahuAkbar! AllahuAkbar!

Nothing describes the happiness of the mu'mineen [faithful] all around the world this day. AllahuAkbar! Our beloved Shaykh is released!" Similarly, on islambase.co.uk, the online home of many British extremists, one member described his release as "the best news in ages." Their attitude suggests that despite the death of Zarqawi and his own long imprisonment, Maqdisi's teachings—a mixture of bigotry and pragmatism—are still seen as relevant. Indeed, Maqdisi's correct predictions in 2004 and 2005 that Zarqawi's attacks on Muslim civilians would undermine support for al-Qaeda both in Iraq and abroad may have further boosted his standing among Islamic extremists worldwide. In light of Maqdisi's influence and popularity it is worth examining his key ideas in detail.

Maqdisi on Takfir

Like many jihadis, Maqdisi's ideology depends on declaring takfir against his Muslim rivals in order to permit violence against them. However, he repeatedly says that declaring takfir should not be undertaken lightly; in his 1997 book This Is Our Aqeedah (creed), he frequently quotes Qadi Iyad, a 12th century judge from Grenada, as saying: "Declaring the blood of those who pray, who are upon tawhid [belief in the unity of God], to be permissible is a serious danger".

Maqdisi adds that takfir should only be pronounced against those who have abandoned tawhid. He says a Muslim abandons tawhid, and hence Islam, if their actions show allegiance to un-Islamic entities by aiding them or participating in their legislation. In other words, he says only those who actively support non-Islamic governments or oppose jihadis should be targeted. Unlike many al-Qaeda members, Maqdisi repeatedly warns on both moral and strategic grounds against pronouncing takfir—and hence carrying out attacks—against ordinary Muslims, saying that in the absence of an Islamic state, it is understandable that many Muslims are unable to perfectly practice Islam.

In his July 2004 book, An Appraisal of the Fruits of Jihad (Waqafat me'a themerat al-jihad), he writes contemptuously of jihadis who "start bombing cinemas or make plans to blow up recreation grounds, sports clubs and other such places frequented by sinful Muslims." Similarly, in This is Our Aqeedah, he criticizes extremists who kill for small infractions of Islamic principles: "The shaving of the beard and imitation of the kuffar (infidel) and other forms of disobedience like it is a general affliction that is spread far and wide. It is not suitable by itself for evidence of takfir."

On Democracy

A large proportion of Maqdisi's writings are devoted to the discussion of democracy, which he regards as one of the main threats to Islam. Maqdisi does not object to democracy as a form of representative government, however, but because legislators deliberately create man-made laws to replace or supplement the sharia (Islamic law).

Maqdisi's arguments stem from his belief that a Muslim's faith is not complete unless he lives under sharia law. As he wrote in his early 1990s book, Democracy is a Religion (Al-Deemoqratiyya Deen): "Obedience in legislation is also an act of worship". Maqdisi consequently argued that anyone seeking to create legislation to replace the sharia is effectively seeking to take the place of God.

From this, he concludes that "anyone who seeks to implement legislation created by someone other than Allah, is in fact a polytheist." Yet his dislike for democracy is not absolute; he accepts that consultation (shura) between a Muslim ruler and his subjects is a valid Islamic principle—but says that this principle has been hijacked by secularists to legitimize the legislative aspect of democracies. Unlike many al-Qaeda fighters, however, Maqdisi says that the illegitimacy of legislative elections does not necessarily permit attacks against anyone who votes, since some people vote only "to choose representatives for worldly living" rather than to subvert the sharia.

On Jihadi Tactics

Maqdisi believes that violent jihad against non-Muslims is a core part of Islam which can be carried out by individuals at any time or place. In an interview with al-Nida magazine in 1999, he described jihad as an "act of worship that is permissible any time".

He also says that jihad is not dependent on living in an Islamist state or having a Caliph, nor is it restricted to battlefields or places of open conflict. Despite this, however, Maqdisi criticizes would-be jihadis whose enthusiasm for glory blinds them to political and religious realities. In An Appraisal of the

Fruits of Jihad, he mocks the "youths moved by their zeal." He continues:

"[They] have studied neither the sharia nor reality. They have newly begun practicing the religion and have not yet rid themselves of the arrogance, pride, and tribalism of their pre-Islamic days, such that some of them even consider it shameful, cowardly, and disgraceful to be secret and discrete. Others proclaim that they are carrying automatic weapons or bombs that they roam about with in their cars here and there, showing them to this person and that person; they think it is a trivial matter to blab to everyone about how they dream and hope to kill Americans and destroy the American military bases in their lands.

They then become astonished at how the enemies of Allah ask him about these things when they interrogate him, and he wonders how they knew about it?!"

Maqdisi also complains that many jihadist attacks are not carried out for strategic benefit but because such attacks are easy:

"*There are other young enthusiasts who oppose us by attacking churches or killing elderly tourists, or relief agency delegates—and other such trivial targets—whereby they do not consider what will benefit the da'wah [call to religion], jihad or Islam, nor do they give preference to what will cause most injury to the enemies of Allah. Rather, their choice is only based on the easiest target.*"

Maqdisi describes the best mujahideen as those who are "*looking for targets that will bring down the enemy combatants and defy them—such as nuclear weapons, or intelligence centers and political posts, or centers of legislation and economy in the land of the polytheists*".

Maqdisi also criticizes those who attack Shiite Muslims, objecting to the attacks on both theological and practical grounds. In a 2005 interview with al-Jazeera, he said that ordinary Shiites could not be held responsible for their beliefs: "*The laypeople of the Shiite are like the laypeople of the Sunna, I don't say 100 percent, but some of these laypeople only know how to pray and fast and do not know the details of the [Shiite] sect*". This pragmatism does not contradict his intellectual hatred for Shiite teachings, saying in This Is Our Aqeedah: "*We declare our hostility toward the path of the Rawafid [the Shiites] who hate the companions of the prophet and curse them.*"

Maqdisi frequently writes that hating non-Muslims is an Islamic duty. In his 1984 book, The Religion of Abraham (Millat Ibrahim), he says that this hatred "*should be shown openly and declared from the outset.*" In *An Appraisal of the Fruits of Jihad*, he writes that any attacks on non-Muslims are theologically justified regardless of whether they result in any progress toward creating, or "consolidating," an Islamic state and regardless of changing political circumstances: "*Any fighting done for the sake of inflicting injury upon the enemies of Allah is a righteous, legislated act, even if it brings about nothing more than inflicting this injury, angering the enemy [and] causing them harm.*"

Simultaneously, however, he argues that for strategic reasons the mujahideen should at present concentrate their efforts on trying to establish a pure Islamic state in the Muslim world, saying that "o*ne of the greatest tragedies of the Muslims today is that they do not have an Islamic state that establishes their religion on the earth.*" He also says that "t*he mammoth, accurately planned operations that were carried out in Washington and New York, despite their size, they do not amount to more than fighting for injury*"— i.e. that they were justified only because they killed non-Muslims but had no strategic benefit. Importantly, however, he also says that if such attacks make it harder for the mujahideen to consolidate and build a true Islamic state, they should be avoided.

Through his writings which simultaneously justify both extreme violence and tactical pragmatism, Maqdisi has gained an iconic status in radical circles at a time when many jihadis—perhaps including even Osama bin Laden and Ayman al-Zawahiri—are becoming increasingly discredited. As a result, a public retraction of his more extreme views would send shockwaves through the jihadist community; on the other hand, a systematic recalibration of jihadist theory focusing attacks on Western military installations and secularists in the Arab world could reinvigorate the jihadi movement and perhaps win it new followers. Given that Jordan has reportedly forbidden Maqdisi from speaking publicly as part of the conditions of his release, it seems unlikely that his views have changed while in prison.

A poem allegedly written by Maqdisi in May 2007 tellingly describes a conversation between himself and the prison authorities in which they tell him: "*Renounce [your views]; many shaykhs have... Renounce and you will be generously rewarded with material [benefits]. In return, you shall [have freedom to] speak*". Maqdisi records his response as "*Prison is sweeter to me ... My suffering for the sake of religion is sweet.*"

If Maqdisi has indeed remained loyal to his ideals, much will depend on how much freedom Jordan's government gives him to propagate his ideas; Maqdisi has consistently shown himself willing to continue promoting jihadist ideology regardless of the personal consequences.

Abu Basir & Abu Qatada

Abu Basir al-Tartusi is another prolific contemporary scholar of Syrian origin. He is a slightly more moderate Salafi ideologue who resides in London, more often criticizing past jihadi mistakes and urging caution and selective action. His tone is due in large part to the scrutiny he was put under following the 2005 London train bombings. He has provided scholarly arguments to back armed resistance to tyrannical rule (*by employing jihadi tactics*), also prefaced on the importance of Muslims living by the Sharia.

Abu Qatada al-Filistini, born in 1960 in the West Bank, is another example of a Palestinian-born cleric who encourages jihad against apostate rule in accordance with the Sharia and is among the most frequently cited authors in the study. His writings contend that, according to the Sharia, it is every Muslim's individual obligation to overthrow and expel any secular government from Muslim lands by bombing, sabotage, coup, or other means available to them that would advance the implementation of Sharia in that land.

These Salafi scholars play a critical but not widely observed role in the global jihadi movement. Ideology is often overlooked and is considered separate from the strategic and operational aspects of Islamist militancy. Yet, the scholars behind the jihadi movement set the framework for debates and provide direction that is by and large adhered to, or is at the least a determining factor in the planning of attacks. By better understanding their role in the movement, governments combating terrorism can attempt to intervene earlier in the radicalization process and ultimately work toward undermining their influence.

The "salafi" conflict

After the war in Iraq started, Zarqawi quickly became one of the most wanted terrorists in the world. As the leader of al-Qa'ida in Iraq, he was involved in the killing of hundreds of Iraqi civilians and the beheading of US citizen Nick Berg before being killed by an American air strike in 2006. These actions were also noticed by other radical Islamists, including Zarqawi's former mentor, Abu Muhammad al-Maqdisi. In 2004 and 2005, the latter criticized Zarqawi for his extreme use of violence. This criticism and the conflict between them that followed are the subject of several academic publicationsas is the claim that al-Maqdisi's critique was a sign of revisionism. The same is true for the arguments between the supporters of the two men and how this conflict led to the establishment of a fatwa council to "protect" jihad from faulty practices.

The division among Salafi-Jihadis in Jordan started in mid-2005 when al-Maqdisi directed an open letter entitled "Munasara wa Munasaha" (Advocating and Advising) to the leader of al-Qaeda in Iraq, Abu Musab al-Zarqawi, criticizing him for targeting Shiite and Christian civilians and accusing al-Zarqawi's organization of being infiltrated by Jordanian security. The shaykh also emphasized the importance of mujahideen leadership being in Iraqi hands.

A few weeks later, al-Zarqawi responded to al-Maqdisi's letter, arguing that the latter's criticism did not have a negative impact on him but instead sabotaged the "jihad in Iraq." These accusations caused divisions to erupt between sympathizers of both parties, a situation intensified by the recent emergence of the so-called the "Neo-Zarqawists."

Similar posts have increased noticeably in jihadi forums, indicating that the division between the "neo-Zarqawists" and the "Maqdisists" is becoming deeper and suggesting that the radical faction of Salafi-Jihadis is growing in Zarqa. Although the mainstream Salafi-Jihadis (as represented by the Maqdisists) are fighting back, the neo-Zarqawists see themselves as inheriting the legacy of Abu Musab al-Zarqawi, which may play a major role in attracting young extremists to this new faction.

Several scholars briefly acknowledge that these discussions and the subsequent rifts between Jordanian radicals after 2004 are rooted in the 1990s, though there is a lack of literature on this period. It was in the 1990s that Zarqawi, Maqdisi, and several other like-minded Jordanians are said to have formed a group known as *Bay'at al-Imam*, or "Fealty to the Leader."

The Syrian Civil War

Initially, Abu Bakr and his senior lieutenants regarded the Syrian uprising as a distraction from its Iraq-centric campaign and they forbade even their Syrian followers from joining the rebellion. However, as the uprising spread and became more violent, they allowed nine Syrian members of the group, headed by Abu Mohammed al Golani, to set up in Northern Syria in mid-2011.

Golani also had the support of Zawahiri, who sent al Qaeda operatives from Pakistan and elsewhere to work with him, and he soon built up an effective fighting force, attracting recruits from both inside and outside the country. The Syrian war went viral, attracting thousands of fighters from around the globe and completely eclipsing the insurgency in Iraq.

Abu Bakr therefore tried to reassert his leadership on both sides of the border and declared that Golani was his subordinate in April 2013. Golani refused to acknowledge that his group Jabhat al Nusra li Ahl al Sham (the Support Front for the People of the Levant) was a branch of The Islamic State of Iraq, and appealed to Zawahiri to rule on the matter, so making public his own association with al Qaeda.

Despite his best efforts over several months, Zawahiri was unable to reconcile the two groups or bring them to arbitration and eventually ordered Abu Bakr to limit his operations to Iraq while appointing Golani al Qaeda's man in Syria. Abu Bakr refused to accept this arrangement and so forced Zawahiri in February 2014 to disavow any al Qaeda connection with The Islamic State of Iraq, which Abu Bakr had already renamed The Islamic State of Iraq and al Sham (ISIS).

With help in particular from Amr al Absi (Abu al Athir al Shami), a Syrian born in Saudi Arabia whose brother had been killed by other rebels while leading a pro-ISIS group in the North of the country, Abu Bakr then set about establishing himself in Syria, drawing away a great many of al Nusra's foreign members.

ISIS quickly became a dominant force in Syria and as well as attracting recruits from al Nusra and other rebel groups, it also received donations and support from outside the area, both as a successful salafist/takfiri group, and as an opponent to the regime of Bashar al Assad.

On 29 June 2014, following rapid territorial gains, which included the capture of Mosul on 10 June, ISIS declared the revival of the Caliphate, naming it The Islamic State and Abu Bakr as Caliph Ibrahim. The declaration was intended as a rallying call to all observant Muslims, but in particular those who shared the salafist/takfiri views expressed by The Islamic State, and so draw away support from like-minded groups in Syria, including al Nusra, that might compete for recruits and resources.

The declaration was also a direct challenge to the authority of Zawahiri and the role of Mullah Omar, who until then had been the undisputed Amir al Mu'minin (Leader of the Faithful). At Friday prayers at the Grand Mosque of al Nuri in Mosul on 4 July 2014, in his first address as Caliph, Abu Bakr claimed that he had reluctantly accepted the title at the behest of the community of Islamic scholars, albeit that they remained unidentified and silent.

The rapid conquest of Mosul and the declaration of the Caliphate caused a brief surge in new recruits,but did not achieve the impact that supporters of The Islamic State had expected or hoped for. Indeed there is evidence to suggest that the reaction among extremists to the declaration of the Caliphate overall was initially negative, though following the start of coalition airstrikes in August 2014, support picked up.

Before declaring the Caliphate, ISIS had conducted some market research through social media to judge the likely reaction. It had also approached several other 'jihadist' groups; for example, Abu Bakr is said to have approached Nasser al Wuhaishi, the military commander of al Qaeda and the head of Al Qaeda in the Arabian Peninsula (AQAP), who - unsurprisingly – rebuffed him. He met a similar response from other leaders though he did receive some support from within Libya, Tunisia, and the Sinai.

Although the consensus opinion was that the declaration of a Caliphate would be premature because the group's control of territory was not yet firm enough, Abu Bakr decided that he had more to gain than to lose, and may also have been deceived by his own appreciation of his historic role.

Jabhat al Nusra has since shown that it faces similar disagreements over raising its status, in this case to become an Islamic Emirate or State. A supposedly leaked tape of Golani announcing an Islamic State in four areas of Syria under al Nusra control on 12 July 2014 was followed by a partial retraction and some confusion.

Although Abu Bakr has failed to achieve a significant number of pledges of allegiance to the Caliphate, even from salafist/takfiri groups, that does not mean that they all oppose him.

Even AQAP has said that it respects the achievements of The Islamic State, even though it does not endorse its claim to leadership. At first the lack of endorsement may have made Abu Bakr appear something of a clown elsewhere in the Muslim world, but his dramatic appearance in Mosul on 4 July, heavy with symbolism that will have impressed some Muslims who watched his performance, and the sheer determination of his fighters in the field, despite the growing alliance against ththem, have at the very least attracted worldwide interest and admiration among extremists.

For example, in July 2014, Abu Bakar Bashir, the leader of salafist/takfiris in Indonesia, announced his support for The Islamic State and was reported by security officials to have been urging his followers to help the movement. Similarly, there has been growing support for The Islamic State in Pakistan and India, where flags and pamphlets with The Islamic State logo are circulating, and even groups closely aligned with al Qaeda acknowledge and praise the objectives and achievements of the self-declared Caliphate.

As Indonesia, Pakistan and India are home to the three largest Muslim communities in the world, it is unsurprising that there are militants among them who are attracted to The Islamic State, but its appeal also reaches into areas where Muslims are an insignificant minority of the population. The mixture of apparent religious legitimacy and military success has proved an inspiration that has drawn recruits and funds from at least 81 countries.

A possible reunification

There are many other salafist/takfiris who sympathize with The Islamic State but are reluctant to break their ties with whatever al Qaeda affiliated organization they have signed up with. They do not welcome the fighting between the two groups, nor the 'with us or against us' attitude of The Islamic State.

As a result, the al Qaeda leadership and many of the senior ideologues that support the salafist/takfiri approach still hope that some reconciliation between the two groups is possible. The coalition airstrikes against The Islamic State, which have also targeted Jabhat al Nusra in Syria and senior al Qaeda members who are there to promote the al Qaeda agenda both in and beyond Syria, has revived attempts to bring the groups together in the face of a common enemy.

These appeals are unlikely to succeed in the short term unless Abu Bakr is recognized as holding some superior position to the leader of any other group, including Zawahiri. But nonetheless, circumstances may yet force the groups to cooperate more closely on the ground. A key factor will be whether The Islamic State is able to maintain the momentum of its recruitment in the face of military reverses and more determined international efforts to estrict its income, impede its movements and prevent its fighters traveling from outside Syria and Iraq.

On the al Qaeda side, while the calls for unity certainly reflect the widespread attitude of its members, they are self-serving in that they remind the audience of the core al Qaeda narrative: that the United States is leading a war against Islam, rather than just against The Islamic State. If, in response to the coalition airstrikes, The Islamic State attempts to launch a major terrorist attack outside Syria and Iraq, it will be seen to have acknowledged the validity of the al Qaeda argument.

Ultimately, the struggle for supremacy between al Qaeda and The Islamic State will turn on two things: the ability of the State to consolidate its territorial gains and hold them over time, and the attitude of the several *thousand foreign fighters who make up over half its core membership. About 15,000 foreigners have joined the Islamic State since 2011, with over half coming from Tunisia, Saudi Arabia, Morocco, Jordan, and Turkey.*

If these fighters desert it, The Islamic State will probably be unable to maintain momentum and so be a far easier target for its enemies. If these fighters join al Qaeda groups, The Islamic State will have to abandon its hopes of dominating the salafist/takfiri environment. But on the other hand, if these fighters stay loyal to The Islamic State but leave Iraq and Syria, The Islamic State will certainly be the dominant force in 'global jihad' for some years to come.

However, its dependence on foreign fighters has shown that The Islamic State has not evolved into a truly indigenous movement, and the very presence of so many foreigners in its ranks may have put local fighters off joining. Certainly they are generally extremely radical and a significant number have become suicide bombers, with The Islamic State reporting suicide attacks in 2014 alone by Afghans, Danes, Egyptians, French, Iranians, Jordanians, Libyans, Moroccans, Pakistanis, Russians (Chechens), Saudi Arabians, Syrians, Tajiks, Tunisians, Turks, and Uzbeks. The great majority of these attacks are carried out by Saudis.

Hamza is back

In an audio message released in August 2015, al-Zawahiri introduced "a lion from the den of al-Qa`ida"—a play on the name Usama, which means "lion" in Arabic.

The next voice on the tape was that of Hamza. He hailed the "martyrdom" of his father and his brother Khalid; praised al-Qa`ida's leaders in Syria, Yemen, and North Africa; lauded the attacks on Fort Hood and the Boston Marathon; and called for jihadis to take the battlefield from Kabul, Baghdad, and Gaza to Washington, London, Paris, and Tel Aviv.

Further statements appeared in May, July, and August 2016, prompting the U.S. State Department in January 2017 to place Hamza on its list of Specially Designated Global Terrorists.

The theme of encouraging attacks on Jewish and Western interests is one to which Hamza has returned again and again in his messages. For example, the first of his May 2017 statements is entitled "Advice for Martyrdom-Seekers in the West."

Over footage of the aftermath of the Fort Hood massacre, a television reconstruction of events leading up to the 1993 World Trade Center bombing, and images connected with other attacks, Hamza encouraged jihadis all over the world to "Sell your soul cheaply for the pleasure of [God]" and urged them to read Inspire magazine, the online publication of al-Qa`ida in the Arabian Peninsula (AQAP) that taught the Boston bombers how to turn a pressure cooker into a weapon.

A caption in the video montage encourages "stabbing with knives and using vehicles and trucks" as an alternative to guns and bombs. Strikingly, Hamza directs followers not to travel to theaters of war within the Muslim world, but instead to attack targets in the West and Russia. "Perhaps you are longing for emigration," he says. "Perhaps you yearn for sacrifice in the battlefields. Know that inflicting punishment on Jews and Crusaders where you are is more vexing and severe for the enemy."

He urges "martyrs" that "the message you intend to convey through your blessed operation must be explained unequivocally in the media" and suggests talking points to align these explanations with al-Qa`ida's own propaganda".

In the same statement, Hamza sets up a hierarchy of targets to be attacked, starting with those who "transgress" against Islam (*such as the editors of the French satirical weekly Charlie Hebdo*), followed by Jewish interests, the United States, other NATO member states, and, lastly, Russia.

It is noteworthy that Hamza accords attacks on Jewish interests a higher priority than those against Americans, whereas Usama bin Ladin in his 1998 fatwa relating to "*Jihad against Jews and Crusaders*" depicted them as coequal targets.

This hierarchy may reflect Hamza's renewed emphasis on the Palestinian cause, dramatically stated in the title of his May 2016 statement, "Jerusalem Is a Bride and Our Blood Is Her Dowry." However, this should not be taken as evidence that al-Qa`ida is about to begin attacking Israel directly. It should be recalled that Usama bin Ladin himself was quite cynical about the matter, admitting privately to his lieutenants that al-Qa`ida's rhetoric about Palestine was no more than "noise" designed to drum up popular support in the Arab world.

The second statement was released during U.S. President Donald Trump's state visit to Saudi Arabia in May 2017, although Hamza does not mention the trip in the text itself. In the latter statement, Hamza reiterates his call for the overthrow of the Saudi monarchy, claiming that the House of Saud has been doing the bidding of foreigners ever since the Kingdom's founder, Ibn Saud, received British aid during World War I.

Hamza's messages frequently repeat, almost word-for-word, sentences uttered by the elder bin Ladin during al-Qa`ida's hey-day in the late 1990s and early 2000s. This tendency can be heard, for example, in Hamza's diatribes on the Palestinian Territories, on what he calls the "occupation" of Saudi Arabia, and on the idea that the United States is "stealing" the wealth of the Muslim world.

In his first statement, Hamza speaks of "following my father" by pledging allegiance to the leader of the Taliban. This is note-worthy in itself; whereas al-Qa`ida's other senior leaders pledge bayat to the emir of the organization (currently al-Zawahiri) who then swears fealty to the Taliban on behalf of al-Qa`ida as a whole, Hamza gives his bayat directly to the Taliban leader, suggesting that, as the heir to bin Ladin, he belongs to a higher class.

Other aspects of the statements confirm the impression that Hamza is being elevated to leadership. In his earlier messages, al-Qa`ida's media arm referred to Hamza as a "Brother Mujahid," a rank-and-file designation. But beginning with his two statements released in May 2017, the organization has started calling him "Sheikh," a title reserved for its topmost brass.

None of Hamza's messages have been accompanied by pictures of the man himself. In fact, the most recent known images are still those of Hamza sifting through helicopter wreckage in the weeks following 9/11, when he was just 12 years old; today, he would be 27 or 28.

When Hamza's first statement came out in August 2015, confidence in al-Zawahiri had reached an all-time low. It had just emerged that Mullah Omar had died in 2013, a year before al-Zawahiri had renewed al-Qa`ida's bayat to the Taliban leader. In other words, either al-Zawahiri had been unaware of Omar's death—in which case he was too far out of the loop to lead—or he had known about it all along and had intentionally sworn allegiance to a dead man—a grave sin in al-Qa`ida's brand of Islam.

This revelation brought dismay and ridicule from jihadis all over the world, at a time when the Islamic State was still capturing all the headlines and attracting the lion's share of recruits. Raising the profile of the heir to bin Ladin was thus an inspired move on the part of al-Zawahiri and the other al-Qa`ida top brass. But Hamza's return will have far broader and longer-term repercussions.

As the Islamic State continues to crumble, many of its adherents will be looking for new banners under which to fight. They are unlikely to pledge allegiance to al-Zawahiri, whom they see as an interloper unworthy of bin Ladin's legacy. It would be an understatement to say that al-Zawahiri lacks the charisma of his predecessor. Moreover, as an Egyptian, he will always struggle to inspire loyalty among other Arabs, especially those from the Arabian Peninsula. Hamza, by contrast, su□ers from none of these handicaps.

His family pedigree, not to mention his dynastic marriage to the daughter of an al-Qa`ida charter member, automatically entitles him to respect from every jihadi who follows bin Ladin's ideology, which includes every Islamic State fighter. As a Saudi descended from prominent families on both his father's and his mother's side, he is well-placed to pull in large donations from patrons in the Gulf, particularly at a time when sectarian fervor is running high in Saudi Arabia.

It is significant in this regard that Hamza has returned to his father's rhetoric castigating the House of Saud. As with bin La-din's 1996 declaration of jihad, this is not just a political message; it is designed to inspire potential donors.

One final aspect of Hamza's messages is noteworthy here. Unlike other leading al-Qa`ida figures, he has never once explicitly criticized the Islamic State. True, he bemoans "strife" between the various groups fighting in Iraq and Syria and calls repeatedly for unity among jihadis to face down what he describes as a "unified enemy" of "Crusaders, Jews, Alawites, rejectionists, and apostate mercenaries." But he carefully avoids naming the self-styled caliphate or its leaders.

The Islamic State, for its part, reciprocates the favor; even as its propaganda castigates al-Zawahiri as a traitor to the cause, it never directly references Hamza. It is significant, too, that many Islamic State supporters who denounce "al-Zawahiri's al-Qa`ida" nevertheless profess admiration for Usama bin Ladin.This is the best evidence that Hamza could be a unifying figure.

It is true that Hamza has never fought on the frontlines—some-thing of which, as is seen in his letters to his father from captivity, he himself is painfully aware. This distinguishes him from the elder bin Ladin, whose warrior myth was built on his exploits against the Soviets in Afghanistan in the 1980s. But it is not as much of a weakness as might be thought. Hamza is not coming out of thin air; he is the favorite son of the most famous jihadi in history. And in a culture where leadership typically descends through a bloodline, pedigree trumps experience.

Moreover, while Hamza has not actually fought, he has been featured in al-Qa`ida propaganda from a very young age, in videos that depict him as having been very close to his father. Perhaps most importantly of all, Hamza clearly has al-Qa`ida's senior leadership behind him.

During his Iranian captivity, Hamza received training from some of al-Qa`ida's top operatives, including al-`Adl and al-Masri. Both of these men are now reportedly free and presumably available to give Hamza their counsel, something bin Ladin himself lacked during the last nine years of his life.

Hamza's ascendancy comes at a moment when al-Qa`ida affiliates are growing in resources and influence across the Islamic world. Al-Nusra, the Syrian franchise now nominally subsumed into Hayat Tahrir al-Sham, may have more than 20,000 militants under its command.

AQAP controls or has a presence in large swathes of Yemen's coastline and highway network. Al-Qa`ida in the Islamic Maghreb recently concluded a merger with several other factions, creating a jihadi conglomerate whose constituent groups collectively carried out over 250 attacks in 2016 alone.

However, since AQAP's threats against U.S. embassies in 2013, these franchises have apparently not sought to use their power to mount attacks against the West. While al-Zawahiri has mostly limited himself to threatening the United States rhetorically, if Hamza takes the reins, there is reason to think that could change, given that his messages repeatedly call for more attacks on American soil, praising previous atrocities like the Fort Hood massacre and the Boston Marathon bombing. As has been seen, Hamza has turned to his father's well-worn anti-American rhetoric, accusing the United States of "occupying" the Arabian Peninsula and "stealing" Muslim wealth.

Many factors suggest that Hamza could be a highly erective leader: his family pedigree, his dynastic marriage, his longstanding jihadi fervor and obvious charisma, and his closeness to al-Qa`ida's most senior operatives. It remains to be seen how, exactly, the organization will make use of him, but it is clear that his star is on the rise. That should worry policymakers in the West as well as in the Muslim world

One day before the 16th anniversary of the 9/11 attacks, Al-Qaeda alerted the world that it would release four messages to coincide with the day the group became the most notorious jihadi group in the world. The post showed the Twin Towers in flames, and the silhouette of a plane approaching. But most interestingly, it depicted two figures in the wreckage of the towers. One is the group's late leader Osama Bin Laden, who masterminded the attack. The second of his son, Hamza bin Laden.

The jihadi's progeny, now in his late twenties, is heir apparent to the ageing leadership of the group that has gained fewer headlines while the Islamic State militant group (ISIS) formed its self-proclaimed caliphate across Iraq and Syria. Bin Laden is being now used as a potent propaganda tool. His name is instantly recognisable to people in the West, as well as the wider jihadi movement.

The U.S. has already designated Hamza as a "global terrorist," a British lawmaker called him the "Crown Prince of Terror," and Al-Qaeda leader Ayman al-Zawahiri introduced him as a "lion from the den" in an August 2015 audio message. Now he is becoming a prominent feature of Al-Qaeda's propaganda output.

As in a previous message from bin Laden's son and likely heir, Hamza bin Laden, Zawahiri again urged jihadist groups to avoid making deals with the enemy, particularly the United States. He warned that while distancing themselves from the larger movement might seem like one way to avoid the full wrath or focus of the U.S. and its partners, it would only end up deceiving the faithful instead.

Zawahiri had supported al-Qaeda's Syrian affiliate Jabhat al-Nusra in May 2016, when it announced it had broken away from al-Qaeda to focus on Syria. Zawahiri's recent change of heart is likely because trying to shed the al-Qaeda label to build local support and blunt massive international pressure hasn't worked for HTS. Instead, HTS is under the most pressure it has ever faced, while suffering as much damage from infighting and defections as from external enemies like the Assad regime, Russia, and the U.S.

Zawahiri further insisted that working with the U.S., for whatever reason, would backfire on any group that tried it, pointing to the Palestinian Authority as a prime example of an organization that gave up everything and got nothing in return.

For Zawahiri, *'you will never be liberated from the clutches of humiliation, subjugation, oppression and corruption unless you engage in an enduring jihad.'* He added that there was no point in trying to avoid being designated a 'global terrorist' by the U.S., so groups might as well start acting like one while cooperating locally to avoid splintering the global movement bin Laden revived.

The honeymoon period for al-Qaeda, in which the so-called Islamic State absorbed most of the counterterrorism focus while al-Qaeda's affiliates grew stronger, is coming to an end. Its affiliates in Yemen and Syria are now under growing pressure. Al-Qaeda's years-long approach of localizing conflicts worked to a degree—but it now appears Zawahiri is seeking to consolidate the terror network and return the group to its heyday as the vanguard of a global movement.

Saif Al Adel

Saif al Adel has been described as one of al-Qa`ida's most effective operatives and one of the few remaining leaders from the pre-9/11 era with the stature to take over from current al-Qa`ida leader Ayman al-Zawahiri. He was born in Monufia Governorate, Egypt.

According to an unconfirmed jihadist account, the Egyptian operative studied business at Shibin el Kom University. At some point during young adulthood, al-`Adl frequented the Fajr al Islam in Shibin el-Kom mosque where he may have become radicalized. The circumstances of his radicalization and decision to join the Egyptian Islamic Jihad (EIJ) are unclear.

By the mid-1980s, al-`Adl was a lieutenant colonel in the Egyptian Special Forces and concurrently involved in Islamist activity aimed at overthrowing the Mubarak regime. On May 6, 1987, he was arrested, along with 6,000 other militants, after an attempted assassination of Interior Minister Hasan Abu Basha. Due to a paucity of evidence against him, al-`Adl was released and promptly demoted. The event precipitated his travel to Afghanistan via Saudi Arabia and, in turn, his decision to join Usama bin Ladin's nascent Arab Afghan organization.

Although al-`Adl was not a founding father of al-Qa`ida (established in August 1988), he played an instrumental role in building the organization's operational capabilities from the ground up. He joined the organization sometime in 1989, where his expertise in military tactics made him an invaluable recruit. During those early years, the former commando served as an instructor in al-Qa`ida training camps in Afghanistan, including Jihad Wahl.

He conducted a "security offensive" course, teaching militants how to carry out abductions and assassinations. According to Nasser al-Bahri, a former bodyguard of Usama bin Ladin, the Egyptian operative directed his students to spend days "studying [their] target's routine: when they ate, where the mosque and canteen were located, how many people were left on guard during prayers and meals, how they organized their rotas."

Furthermore, al-`Adl helped al-Qa`ida formulate doctrines in target assessment and intelligence collection that strengthened the organization's operational capabilities.Given the Egyptian operative's in-demand skill sets, he quickly ascended the al-Qa`ida hierarchy. By the mid-1990s, al-`Adl became the head of al-Qa`ida's security committee, part of the security detail for bin Ladin and Muhammad Atef's (Abu Hafs al Masri) right-hand man in the military committee.

Al-`Adl played an important role in the establishment of al-Qa`ida's infrastructure in the Horn of Africa, particularly Somalia. In 1993, he traveled, along with senior Egyptian al-Qa`ida operative Abu Muhammad al Masri, via Kenya to Ras Kambooni in Somalia to establish a training camp.

There, al-`Adl developed good relations with the Ogadan tribe, aligned with Somali warlord Farah Aideed's faction. The infrastructure in Ras Kambooni was subsequently utilized as a base to conduct raids on peacekeeping forces in the region. As Abu Walid al Masri, al-`Adl's father-in-law, put it in a letter to him and other al-Qa`ida operatives at the time, *"The American bald eagle has landed within range of our rifles. You can kill it or leave it permanently disfigured,"* an ominous turn of phrase indicating al-Qa`ida's willingness to take on American forces in the region.

In 1999, al-`Adl met with Abu Musab al-Zarqawi, who had just been released from Jordanian imprisonment for his role in an attempt on the life of an American diplomat in Amman.

After hearing reports of al-Zarqawi's arrival in Kandahar, Afghanistan, and conferring with the radical preacher Abu Qatada al Falistini, al-`Adl along with a colleague met al-Zarqawi in a guesthouse there. The Egyptian operative found that he had a great deal in common with al-Zarqawi, including an "uncompromising" nature. The following morning, al-`Adl convinced bin Ladin, despite his reservations over the Jordanian operative's refusal to swear *bay`a*, to invest in al-Zarqawi's nascent *Tawhid* organization. By providing money, al-Zarqawi was able to establish a training camp in Herat, near the Afghanistan-Iran border.

The decision to establish a training camp and smuggling routes proved to be fortuitous. It was becoming increasingly more arduous for militants to travel to Afghanistan via Pakistan because of a Pakistani crackdown on Arab Afghan activity. Two al-Qa`ida stations in Tehran and Mashad were established to facilitate travel to and from Afghanistan. In the aftermath of 9/11, al-`Adl likely used the same routes to smuggle al-Qa`ida operatives into Iran.

According to testimony provided to the U.S. government by Khaled Sheikh Muhammad, lead planner of the 9/11 attacks, in the spring of 1999 Usama bin Ladin and Muhammad Atef approved the attack plans that evolved into the 9/11 attacks. Al-`Adl was informed of the plot sometime in April 2001. According to the 9/11 Commission, al-`Adl was part of a faction within al-Qa`ida that had reservations about the plot because they feared it could endanger the position of the Taliban.

On June 13, 2002, al-`Adl wrote in a private communiqué to Khalid Sheikh Muhammad to "stop rushing into action and take time out to consider all the fatal and successive disasters that have afflicted us during a period of no more than six months."

He went on to disparage bin Ladin as an ineffective leader who did not accept dissent. *"If someone opposes him, he immediately puts forward another person to render an opinion in his support, clinging to his opinion and totally disregarding those around him."* In his treatise on Security and Intelligence, al-`Adl made a similar point. He argued that when an enemy continues to inflict heavy losses on a jihadist organization, it is necessary for the *shabaab* (youth) to refrain from action and regroup. In short he was critical of any rush to action devoid of careful cost-benefit analysis.

Despite his private dissatisfaction with the results of the 9/11 attacks, publicly al-`Adl towed the party line. He claimed in his 2005 biography of al-Zarqawi that the "ultimate objective" of the planes operation "against the head of the snake was to prompt it to come out of its burrow," and this had been partially achieved.

In other words, the aim of the operation was to provoke imperial overreach on the part of the United States, by instigating an invasion of Afghanistan and subsequently Iraq. It is possible that al-Qa`ida's restored fortunes and growing presence in Iraq had made him reconsider his previous position.

Al-`Adl argued that the American bombardment of al-Qa`ida installations in Afghanistan during Operation Enduring Freedom served two principal aims: to put an end to the Islamic Emirate of Afghanistan and eliminate the al-Qa`ida hierarchy.

In recognition of American aims, he outlined how al-Qa`ida evacuated its personnel and did its utmost to salvage what remained of its network in Afghanistan. In the aftermath of the fall of Kandahar in December 2001, al-`Adl led a cohort of al-Qa`ida operatives to Iran transiting via a network of safe houses.

When he and Abu Muhammad al Masri arrived in Iran, al-`Adl reestablished contact with al-Qa`ida's senior leadership in the Afghanistan-Pakistan region and sent operatives to Afghanistan to carry out operations. He may have played an operational role in the May 2003 Riyadh compound bombings, albeit a circumscribed one because of his imprisonment, which began a month earlier.

Saudi and American pressure had led Tehran to imprison al-`Adl along with Abu Muhammad al-Masri. Thereafter, al-`Adl's operational involvement diminished precipitously, though he remained able to publish articles online occasionally.

By the mid-2000s, al-Qa`ida Central was infuriated by al-Zarqawi's sectarian campaign against Iraqi Shiites, creating a public relations quagmire for the organization. In December 2005, Attiyat Abdul Rahman al-Libi reprimanded al-Zarqawi in a scathing letter, which suggested his brutal and unrestrained targeting of the Shia was endangering the entire brand.

It is unclear where al-`Adl stood on the schism between bin Ladin and al-Zarqawi due to a lack of primary source documentation on the subject. Given he had been an early champion al-Zarqawi and praised him in the 2005 biography, the growing tension must have been awkward for al-`Adl.

Interestingly, al-`Adl raised ideas that the Islamic State would later champion. In contrast to bin Ladin's more methodical approach to an Islamic caliphate, al-`Adl wrote that he had advised al-Zarqawi that circumstances were appropriate for the declaration of an Islamic state.

Al-Qa`ida leaders were still holding out hope that al-`Adl might be released but recognized that even under the best of circumstances, it would take time for him to return to the fray. After bin Ladin's death there were reports al-`Adl took over in a caretaker capacity before Ayman al-Zawahiri was appointed leader, but this was not confirmed by the terrorist organization.

Few operatives in al-Qa`ida Central elicit as much concern within the intelligence community as al-`Adl. The Egyptian operative has served several roles within the organization, including military trainer, head of Usama bin Ladin's security detail, and head of al-Qa`ida's security committee. Al-`Adl has demonstrated an uncanny capacity to adapt to changing circumstances, for example not only surviving over a decade of imprisonment in Iran but using it to lengthen his career.

Zarqawi's biographer

« All praise is to Allah, Lord of the worlds. Prayers and peace be upon the Master of Apostles, the Imam of the pious, the Leader of al-Mujahideen, upon His family, His companions, and all those who follow them in righteousness until the day of resurrection.

I have never been a hobbyist of reading or writing, nor have I been a fan of rhetoric. However, due to the circumstances that I am experiencing nowadays, I found myself having plenty of free time which I spent in performing al-Zikr, memorizing al-Qur'an, and doing some physical exercises. In this daily routine of mine, I received your request to write about my experience with the dear brother, Abu Mus'ab (Ahmad Fadil).

I was reluctant at the beginning, but after performing al-Istikhara, I felt at ease. Therefore, memories and thoughts began to flow into my mind, one after another. I pray to Allah Almighty, the Lord of the Great Throne, to count this effort of mine as one of my good deeds and to make it useful to my brothers, the free Mujahideen everywhere.

I follow the news of their Jihad and victories with much yearning and pride. They are the lions and heroes of this Ummah; they are its hope, the right choice, and the vanguards on the path of glory, dignity, victory, and empowerment, by Allah's permission. I consider my brother Abu Mus'ab as one of the best among those heroic lions, and Allah is his Assessor.

After Allah granted al-Mujahideen in Afghanistan a manifest victory over the infidels, the polytheist Russians and apostates, and after discord among the Afghan factions began to surface, many of our Arab brothers began to think of returning back to their native countries, particularly the Saudi, Yemeni, and Jordanian brothers who had no security issues with their countries.

On the other hand, we, the Egyptians, and our Syrian, Algerian, and Libyan brothers had no alternative but to stay in Afghanistan or to move to other hot Jihad fronts, or to move to safer places where there were no strong central governments, and in which we have strong alliances on the ground.

Thus was our choice to move to Sudan, Somalia, and some underprivileged African countries. Some of our brothers had already moved to the countries which gained independence from the collapsed Soviet Union. Some others wandered all over the world. Meanwhile, some truthful and seasoned brothers viewed that this exodus was a major loss and expeditious steps had to be taken to stop it to save what can be saved. They urged that the potential and energy instilled in these truthful great souls must be gathered, organized, and put to use to make the desired change.

Thus, the idea of the blessed Qaeda al-Jihad emerged as a preliminary step on this path. We began to collect needed information to restructure our action. One of the priorities was to obtain recent and old information on all the pioneers of al-Jihad who participated in al-Jihad in Afghanistan. On top of the list of those pioneers on whom information must be updated were our Jordanian and Palestinian brothers.

This is why we were following closely the military tribunals which were held by the Jordanian State Security Court for our brothers, the Jordanians who returned from Afghanistan, and for the various small Islamic groups which were attempting to carry out some Jihadist activities against the state of the Zionist enemy in beloved Palestine from the Jordanian soil. At the top of the list in the media spectrum were brothers Abu Muhammad al-Maqdisi and Abu Mus'ab.

This is so because of the sessions of their trial in the case of al-Tawhid, or Bay'at al-Imam (Allegiance to the Imam). Our brother, Omar Abu Omar, (Abu Qutada) was keen on publishing the writings of those two brothers in his magazine al-Minhaj, which was published in London, in addition to their historical defenses before the judges of the court. Brother Abu Qutada al-Filistini used to assure us that we have good brothers who are active in Jordan, and that they have a bright future in the path of the blessed Da'wa.

We were very happy when we learned of their release in the beginning of the year 1999. We were not surprised when we were told that brother Abu Mus'ab, along with some of his brothers, arrived in Pakistan. I say we were not surprised since the idea to join al-Mujahideen and to come to its aid anywhere is the duty of everyone who has sound understanding of true Islam and its Aqida.

The information we had indicated that the intention of Abu Mus'ab was to go to Chechnya, for it was the hottest and the most appealing arena then. If we try to analyze this information, it would lead us to the conclusion that Abu Mus'ab was of a higher degree of awareness and sincerity regarding his inclinations.

His willingness to go to Chechnya meant that he was ready to sacrifice for his beliefs. The desired change in the situation of al-Ummah would not be achieved by mere wishes, theory of inevitable victory, or hypothetical power alone. Rather it requires a real and sincere practice by those ideologues.

al-Ummah's masses would not be fooled anymore. They would not run behind everyone who crowed. They became aware that a tangible change in their lives was the only thing that could influence them. Accordingly, the philosophy of al-Qaeda merged to address al-Ummah's masses on this foundation. I will elaborate on this point later, by Allah's permission.

Meanwhile, Abu Mus'ab and his two companions faced problems with the Pakistani security services regarding their residence permits. The brothers were taken into custody, but there was an agreement to release them on the condition that they leave Pakistan. Abu Mus'ab and his two companions had no other choice but to go to Afghanistan.

Similarities Between Me and Abu Mus'ab:

I received reports on the arrival of a group of Jordanians to Kandahar. I was busy attending to some duties outside the city. I returned to Kandahar two weeks after the arrival of Abu Mus'ab. Then I headed to meet him in the guesthouse which was earmarked to accommodate guests and newcomers. Both Abu Mus'ab and Abu Muhammad al-Maqdisi did not need a Tazkiya (previous recommendation) to us as their news on the sessions of the military tribunal which were held for both of them in Jordan, and their views which they made public during the trials, were satisfactory enough.

Earlier, Abu Qutada and one of Shuyoukh al-Jihad in Jordan spoke well of both of them. I should mention here that I met with the brother who was responsible for following up on Abu Mus'ab and his two companions. I wanted to be in the picture regarding what happened between Abu Mus'ab and the brothers.

The final conclusion was as follows: Abu Mus'ab holds hard-line views on some issues over which no agreement was concluded. This stirred my anger and opened the door wide for personal memories which evoked most of the important phases in my history and relations, after I was guided by Allah to understand the true Islam in the early 1980s.

Owing to these memories, I found pre-justification for Abu Mus'ab before meeting him. I arrived at Abu Mus'ab's place of residence after al-Maghrib prayer. I was accompanied by an Egyptian brother who used to have affiliations with al-Gama'a al-Islamiya in Egypt. Shaykh Abdulakhar (Hammad al-Ghunaymi) was his Shaykh in the past. As a result of some acts and ideas, this brother was not in full agreement with other Shuyoukh in some of organizational and practical Ijtihadat.

As we entered the guesthouse, Abu Mus'ab and both his companions were at the door to welcome us since I notified them of my arrival two hours in advance. We hugged the brothers and congratulated them on their safe arrival. When we entered the guesthouse we found that the men were down to earth. We introduced ourselves briefly and began to talk.

I found that I was talking to a man with whom I shared many traits. Abu

Mus'ab was a sturdy man who was not really very good with words. He expressed himself spontaneously and briefly. He would not compromise any of his beliefs. He was uncompromising but he had a clear objective, which he strove to achieve the re-establishment of true Islam in society. He did not have details regarding how to achieve this objective except for initiating al-Tawheed comprehending the true Aqida, and initiating al-Jihad against al-Ummah's enemy. Abu Mus'ab's life experience was not very rich. He had, however, great ambitions and defined goals. I asked him in detail about the situation in Jordan and Palestine.

He had adequate information about Jordan, but his information about Palestine was very poor. Then we discussed points of disagreement between him and the brothers. We listened to him, but we did not argue since we wanted to win him over to our side in the first place. Our meeting lasted for five straight hours, during which we listened to all he had to say. We left them and promised to meet again in two days.

The next morning, I was scheduled to meet with both Shaykh Osama Bin Ladin and Shaykh Ayman al-Zawahiri, may Allah protect them. We had a planned agenda to discuss, after which I suggested that we talk about Abu Mus'ab since the brothers were already well informed about the issue.

The controversial issues with Abu Mus'ab were not new or uncommon. We used to have some disagreements with hundreds of other brothers who came from various regions in the world regarding certain issues. The reason was the diverse understanding of some aspects of al-Aqida that pertain to the al-Walaa and the al-Baraa, and the subsequent issues of al-Takfir or al-Irjaa. Other controversial issues included a modus-operandi and how to cope with the current circumstances, each in his surroundings and home country.

The most important issue with Abu Mus'ab was the stance regarding the Saudi regime and how to deal with it in light of the Islamic laws that pertain to al-Kufr and al-Iman.

I suggested to the brothers that they could entrust me to handle these cases, including Abu Mus'ab's and similar cases. It was both unfair - in terms of al-Fiqh -and incorrect - in terms of the organizational build up - to abandon every brother or group with whom we might have minor disagreements.

Delegation from Bin Ladin and al-Zawahiri:

The information we had in al-Qaeda and its Manhaj that we did not have many supporters in Palestine or Jordan. The plan that the brothers agreed on underlined the importance of the presence of al-Qaeda in

Jordan and Palestine, since the Palestinian issue is the bleeding heart of al-Ummah. Thus, everyone who wanted to be close to al-Ummah's sentiments should be in touch with this issue. The liberation of al-Ummah is contingent on dealing a strike to the Israelis and annihilating their state. There will be no change or liberation unless Israel is undermined and eliminated.

The survival of the regional order was linked to the survival of the state of Israel. The regional order existed in favour of Israel's ambitions to pave the way for its expansion. The relationship between the current Arab regime and the state of Israel was dialectical. We were in agreement that there would be no liberation without change and no change unless Israel was weakened. Israel would not be weakened unless Arab regimes were undermined and unless Western support for Israel and these regimes came to a halt.

The logical conclusion, therefore, was that it is imperative for us to be present on this globe. So, how could we abandon such an opportunity to be in Palestine and Jordan? And how could we waste a chance to work with Abu Mus'ab and similar brothers in other countries? Following two hours of non-stop discussion, the brothers agreed to designate me to handle this issue while providing me with the means to do so.

I praised Allah Almighty for this success since this issue has been a source of worry for me for more than 10 years. I myself was not in full agreement with everyone, particularly regarding tactical and strategic aspects. This problem surfaced since the first day I was detained in Egypt on May 6, 1987 regarding the case of the reestablishment of al-Jihad movement and a coup attempt.

The case was known as al-Jihad 401 in which nearly 6,000 brothers were arrested. Up to 417 of them remained in custody. The case pertained to the assassination attempt against ex-Egyptian Interior Minister Hassan Abu Basha and a journalist, Makram Muhammad Ahmad. I was then a lieutenant colonel in the Egyptian Special Forces.

Major Muhammad al-Barm of the Special Forces and Special Guard, may Allah protect him and grant him success, was with me. I found that the brothers at al-Jihad movement and al-Gama'a al-Islamiya lacked practical experience that could enable them to achieve the desired change. In my opinion and the opinion of some brothers, this was due to over-enthusiasm that resulted in hasty action or recklessness at times. Moreover, they lacked the necessary expertise, a short-term and long-term plan in advance, and a vision to employ al-Ummah's human resources, not physical resources, at the highest level.

Change required an ideology, human resources, funds, and sincere, experienced, and seasoned leadership that possessed a vision and a plan, which would define its goals and means. The banner of such leadership should be clear.

The reasons that prompted me to leave Egypt in the aftermath of the above-mentioned case were very similar to the reasons that prompted Abu Mus'ab to leave Jordan. These identical reasons included the following:

1. The Egyptian and Jordanian security services began to realise that the major threat to the regime was ideological Islamic groups who did not believe in middle solutions and who called for a radical and comprehensive change in the political, economic, social, and ideological fronts. Accordingly, the security services were monitoring Islamic movements day and night. They were trying to deal preemptive strikes to them to deny them an opportunity to go ahead with the process of calm and constructive buildup.

2. The security services in both Egypt and Jordan began to recruit informers within these groups. They succeeded in this field to a large extent for many reasons that we would not mention in this article. Consequently, we felt it was important that the leadership of an Islamic action should be remote from these strikes to enable it to plan effectively and achieve its plans.

3. There was a lack of necessary local financial resources in both countries to achieve the desired Islamic change. It was necessary, therefore, to knock on foreign doors in search of substantial funding.

4. Communication and integration with trustworthy Islamic individuals and groups would never take place as long as merciless security services existed in these countries. Departure, therefore, was a must.

5. Support for hot Islamic issues. A free and honest person would not stay still seeing his family and his Ummah suffer injustice and humiliation.

The aforementioned reasons prompted me and Abu Mus'ab to leave our countries and head to the open arenas of al-Jihad in the Islamic world. After the two Shaykhayn, may Allah protect them, approved to designate me to handle the case of Abu Mus'ab and similar cases, I contacted some brothers whom I trusted their intellectual ability and vast practical experience. We held an emergency meeting during which we discussed the issue from all aspects. We made important decisions after our nine-hour meeting during which we performed prayers and had a meal.

I had a complete and clear perspective of a new and enormous project. The preliminary success of the project was linked to the approval of Abu Mus'ab. I make dua for Allah to help me to convince Abu Mus'ab of this partial plan which is would be vital for the greater Islamic project that we were striving to accomplish. We scheduled a meeting with Abu Mus'ab for 09:00 AM the next morning. I left with the Egyptian brother whom I mentioned before. We both went with one Jazrawi brother. He was from al-Hijaz and he had a long experience in issues of al-Jihad and the Islamic action in various fields. He was in full agreement with me regarding most issues.

This time, we did not enter the guesthouse. We asked Abu Mus'ab to accompany us alone. He got in the car and we headed to the home of the Hijazi brother. We introduced Abu Mus'ab to the man and I felt that Abu Mus'ab was happy to meet him.

I began the conversation since I was the proponent of the project. I had a thorough idea of its aspects and goals. The main idea of the project was based on the importance of finding an area in Afghanistan where a simple camp would be established for daily training. Abu Mus'ab would oversee the camp and bring in brothers from Jordan, Palestine, Syria, Lebanon, Iraq, and Turkey to forge a presence for us in these important areas.

The second point that we discussed earlier with some experts was it is important that such an area would be remote from our headquarters and would be located on the western border of Afghanistan adjacent to Iran. This is so because Iran became a safe passage for the brothers after the Pakistani authorities began to tighten the noose around our movement. It was very difficult for Arab and other brothers to arrive in Afghanistan through Pakistan. It was easy, on the other hand, for the brothers to take the Turkey to Iran to Afghanistan route.

Herat was suitable and the nearest Afghan city to the Iranian border and it was somewhat remote from us. Arrival to and departure from the city was much easier. Concerning financial resources, the Hijazi brother and some of his companions promised to make the resources available to accommodate the human resources in Herat and the requirements of the course of action.

One of the topics we discussed was that we were not seeking full Bay'a from Abu Mus'ab or his companions. Rather, we wanted coordination and cooperation to achieve our joint objectives. We explained to him that we were ready to provide him with special training for every distinguished individual or group from his side.

We pledged to coordinate with the brothers of the Taliban movement to avoid any obstacles in the future. We proposed the establishment of two stations in Tehran and Mashhad in Iran to facilitate arrival in and departure of brothers to and from Afghanistan. The objective was integration of an important region in the Arab and Islamic world. It would provide an opportunity for every sincere brother, particularly those who did not fully agree with the Manhaj of the al-Qaeda, to achieve integration at the current stage and full agreement in the near future, by Allah's permission.

We tried to obtain an immediate response from Abu Mus'ab, but he said: "I have to carry out some consultations. My brothers Khalid al-'Aruri and Abdulhadi Dughlas have accompanied me from the beginning and I should consult with them". We agreed to meet in two days. It would be a Friday. The Hijazi brother invited us for lunch on that day. Everyone agreed and Abu Mus'ab was told to bring both his companions for lunch.

We agreed to send a car for them before Friday prayers so that we could perform prayers together. Two days later, we performed al-Jumu'a prayer together and went to the home of the Hijazi brother. We had Arabic Kabsa for lunch. Abdulhadi inquired about certain issues. His questions indicated he was quite intelligent. Allah Almighty granted us the ability to answer all their questions.

The result was total approval from Abu Mus'ab and his two companions. We agreed to begin preparations as of the next day. The plan stipulated that Abu Mus'ab and his two companions would spend 45 days in special training while we would make the necessary arrangements in Herat and Mashhad consecutively. Abu Mus'ab began to contact his friends to urge them to come.

During the training, I noticed that Abu Mus'ab and both his companions were very enthusiastic about the training. They worked very hard to achieve the highest levels. The training period went by quickly and we began to prepare to move to Herat in harmony with the plan. Meanwhile, two Syrian brothers arrived. We discussed the Herat plan with them and they agreed without hesitation.

Then we moved to Herat where we found that the brothers chose an area on the outskirts of Herat where there was an old and small camp, which they provided with the necessary supplies. We praised Allah Almighty for this success. We stayed in Herat with them for four days after which I felt that Abu Mus'ab and his Jordanian and Syrian comrades are in full agreement in thoughts with us. We agreed to meet every month.

They would come to us one month and we would visit them the next. We left with them three vans that escorted us in our trip. We promised to send more cars if necessary. We saw them off and returned to our location. We left Abu Mus'ab with his two companions, Khalid and Abdulhadi, and the Syrian brothers. We were confident they would succeed and excel in their project since every one of them had a very strong will. Their concern for Islam and Muslims was unparalleled. When we arrived at our headquarters, we submitted a detailed report to the brothers. I felt that they were satisfied with the achievement that was made.

A full month passed since we returned from Herat during which we prepared three vans and loaded them with supplies that we believed the brothers there would need. I left with five Arab companions including the aforementioned Hijazi brother. We accompanied two Afghan brothers. We arrived in Herat late in the afternoon.

We informed Abu Mus'ab in advance about the time of our arrival. The brothers were waiting for us. They prepared lunch of various dishes, mostly Shami dishes. The meal was delicious. It was different from the food we used to have during the four days that we spent in Herat last month. When I inquired, I was told that two Syrian families, originally from Aleppo who used to live in Turkey and who arrived in Herat five days ago, prepared the lunch. I was glad to hear the news since it meant that the idea was finding its way to success. I was grateful to Allah.

We began to inquire about the conditions and difficulties that faced them over the past month and the achievements they made.

The outcomes were as follows:

1. *Abu Mus'ab and his comrades were able to bolster relations with Taliban officials in the area. Taliban men were ready to provide all the resources at their disposal in favor of the project.*

2. *There were five people when we left Herat the first time, Abu Mus'ab, his two companions, and the two Syrian brothers. We found that the two Syrian families who came to Herat comprised 13 members including the head of the family, three young men over 16, two women, and six girls. In all, the number of Arabs in Herat amounted to 18.*

3. *We found that in cooperation with the Syrian brothers, Abu Mus'ab prepared a military and cultural program that I thought was remarkable. The cultural program focused on al-Aqida, memorizing al-Qur'an, and studying history and geography.*

4. We found that Abu Mus'ab and his companions agreed to form the structure of an integrated society in light of their expectations that hundreds of brothers and their families would join them in Herat soon.

5. We learned that Abu Mus'ab sent a note to his brothers in Jordan telling them of the beginning of his success in Afghanistan and asking them to immigrate there if they could. He asked if his family and the families of Abdulhadi and Khalid could join them. The Syrian brothers did the same and this indicated they were confident that the project would succeed.

We praised Allah for this magnificent progress. We discussed developments regarding an increase in the resources and the stations of Mashhad and Istanbul. We spent three days during which we took part in their daily program. We noticed the enthusiasm and sincerity that prevailed. We saw them off and agreed that they would come to visit us after one month. We returned to our headquarters happy and optimistic. The Hijazi brother was seriously thinking of joining Abu Mus'ab and his companions in Herat. We updated our information of the Herat file that we opened three months ago. We briefed the brothers concerned about the developments.

A Mini Islamic Society:

The days passed quickly and the date of our monthly meeting arrived. Abu Mus'ab and his Syrian brother, Abu al-Ghadiya, came carrying good news. The number in the camp amounted to 42 men, women, and children including the families of Abu Mus'ab and his two companions. Three new Syrian families arrived including one that came from Europe. Abu Mus'ab was optimistic that they were establishing a mini Islamic society. He said that Jordanian and Palestinian brothers would arrive in Herat soon. He said the Iran-Afghanistan route was safe to travel.

This passage was new and important to us in the al-Qaeda. We took advantage of it later on. We used it instead of the old route through Pakistan, particularly for the passage of Arab brothers. This issue prompted us to think of building good relations with some virtuous people in Iran to pave the way and coordinate regarding issues of mutual interest.

Coordination with the Iranians was achieved later. Coordination was made with sincere individuals who were hostile to the Americans and the Israelis. It was not made with the Iranian government.

During this time, I noticed a significant development in Abu Mus'ab's *characters. When we first met four months ago, he was not the one who would begin a conversation. His ideas and interests in political news were limited. Now, however, he was the one who would start a conversation. He was interested in every issue. He would utilize public relations that might lead his project to success. I noticed that he became more convincing and influential when he spoke to someone.*

He spoke more in standard Arabic, whereas before he used to speak in his normal dialect. All these points indicated that he would become a distinguished leader. His Syrian companion was wonderful. He possessed vast experiences and mastered several languages including English, Turkish, and some Kurdish. The Syrian brothers whom I got to know in Afghanistan were the most sincere people I have ever met.

The suffering they faced and still face played a great role in shaping their personality. They were respectful and obedient to their leaders. They were motivated to learn and gain academic and practical experience. I was satisfied with Abu Mus'ab's project whenever I learned that new numbers of brothers were joining him.

Abu Mus'ab's project was making progress in terms of the number of brothers of various nationalities who converged on Herat to join him. These included Syrians, Jordanians, Palestinians, and some Lebanese and Iraqis. All praise is to Allah, Abu Mus'ab was able to build relations with the Kurdish Ansar al-Islam, which is active in northern Iraq and had bases and clear presence there.

We continued to pay periodic visits to Herat. Every time, we could notice the progress at the organizational and administrative levels and the military capabilities of the young men. At the dawn of 2001, Abu Mus'ab became a different person in terms of resources and the potential he possessed. His perspective and thoughts became more profound concerning every issue he faced.

He began to plan for the future in a strategic manner. He focused on building relations with all nationalities and races including young Arab and non-Arab men in the Afghan arena. He traveled in Afghanistan to meet with them and listen to the news of their countries of origin. Most of the time, he left Abdulhadi Dughlas as his deputy in Herat.

He used to travel with Khalid al-'Aruri and Sulayman Darwish Abu al-Ghadiya. I could say that Abu Mus'ab's comprehensive leadership qualities became obvious, with the characteristics based on the following points:

1. He was concerned about the situation of the entire Islamic Ummah.

2. *Dedication, accuracy, and his attempt to achieve swift results became the most visible of his traits.*

3. *He became fond of reading and was always interested in everything that took place in the world.*

4. *He was a fan of Nourddine Zinki, a distinguished Islamic leader who led the process of liberation and change that was completed by the hero Salahuddine al-Ayyubi. Abu Mus'ab always asked if there were books available about Nourddine and Salahuddine. I think that the books Abu Mus'ab read about Nourddine, who launched his campaign from Mosul in Iraq, influenced him to move to Iraq in the aftermath of the downfall of the Islamic Emirate of Afghanistan.*

5. Abu Mus'ab became more concerned about the situation of the individuals around him. He often discussed with me the means that would strengthen their social and psychological relations. The story of the marriage of the Prophet, to Aysha and Hafsa, the daughters of his friends, Abu Bakr and Omar, were a model to him.

Abu Mus'ab married one of the daughters of his Palestinian companions who joined him from Jordan. Abu Mus'ab's friends got married and so were their daughters although some of the girls were at young age compared to the age of their peers who get married in our Arab world.

Abu Mus'ab and his brothers became one family in terms of religion and social and economic relations. They lived in an atmosphere of friendship reminiscent of the atmosphere that prevailed between the apostle, and his companions. This modern example should be a lesson for everyone who works in the field of al-Da'wa and the contemporary Islamic movement.

6. After spending two years in Herat, Abu Mus'ab began to think of dispatching his trustworthy companions to areas outside Afghanistan to recruit young men and collect funds. As I remember, the beginning was in Turkey and Germany since the Syrian brothers who joined him had good relations in both countries.

7. Among the brothers I have met, Abu Mus'ab was one of the most determined to protect the honour, blood, and reputation of Muslims.

These were some of the characteristics of Abu Mus'ab prior to the events of September, 11 2001.

Goals of New York Strike:

In the meantime, we at al-Qaeda made preparations to carry out the greater strike. Our goals focused on the following three points: more than two centuries of human history, the United States has gone on the rampage everywhere in the world. It was intimidating and assaulting people.

It was seizing the resources of nations. Some people might be surprised if we tell them that the United States sent its fleet to occupy Algeria in 1817. al-Mujahideen and Arab sailors in the Mediterranean, whom the West labeled as pirates, confronted and defeated the US fleet. The battles between the US and Islamic parties lasted for more than three months. That US aggression was the prelude to implementing the colonialist plan, which was endorsed at the second conference of European nations held in Vienna in 1815.

Since then, the United States has been trying hard to attack our Ummah to intimidate it and seize its resources. It has been humiliating all the beleaguered people in the world. Over the past century, the United States was trying to intimidate China, Korea, and Vietnam. It conspired against nations in Africa and South America. The objective was clear: a flagrant and atrocious aggression established on pretexts that have always been shrouded with deception. The United States overthrew several governments.

The events that took place in Yugoslavia were fresh in memory. The United States assassinated many of the world's leaders who were opposed to it. It spared no means to achieve its goals. Nevertheless, no state or country in the world dared to retaliate for the US aggression.

The prejudice and arrogance of the United States dominated its psychological makeup, which fuelled its injustice to the extent that it looked down on other nations and people. Our main objective, therefore, was to deal a strike to the head of the snake at home to smash its arrogance. This objective was partially achieved, all praise is to Allah. Had the other strikes succeeded the way the strike against the two towers did, the world would have felt the sudden change.

> 2. *The second objective of this strike was to declare a new virtuous leadership for this world, which was crushed under the feet of the Zionist-Anglo-Saxon-Protestant coalition. Our vision said that genuine Muslims are the only ones who possess the qualifications needed to lead humankind and save it from the darkness of injustice and aggression of the wicked coalition.*

Our Ummah and the beleaguered people of the world will realise that there are people who do not fear this satanic coalition and that the newcomers possess a well examined plan to change the miserable life of the underprivileged in the world. These newcomers will become the virtuous leadership of this globe that will face the forces of evil and injustice.

The divine rule governing the conflict is And say, truth has arrived, and falsehood perished: for falsehood is by its nature bound to perish. Truth will prevail. It will fight falsehood and defeat it sooner or later. The slogan we have adopted regarding this issue is the statement of Rab'i ibn Amir when he met Rustum, the Persian leader, before the Battle of al-Qadisiya.

Rustum asked him why he came. and worship the Lord of the human race. He sent us to save people from the injustice of religions to the justice of Islam and from the hardship of the world to relief of the world and the hereafter". A free person does not accept agony for himself, his family, or the entire human race. How do we keep silent against this flagrant injustice and blatant negligence of human values and the legacy that was desecrated by these abnormal people?

Our objective is the emergence of a sincere and virtuous Islamic leadership that rallies al-Ummah's capabilities and motivates the weak and deceived in this world against this octopus that is represented by this wicked coalition. Such leadership says what it believes in and does what it says. It fears Allah alone. Nothing but Allah's destiny will turn it away from achieving its goals.

All praise is to Allah, this has been accomplished.

3. *Our ultimate objective of these painful strikes against the head of the snake was to prompt it to come out of its burrow. This would make it easier for us to deal consecutive blows to undermine it and tear it apart. It would foster our credibility in front of our Ummah and the beleaguered people of the world.*

A person will react randomly when he receives painful strikes on his head from an undisclosed enemy. Such strikes will force the person to carry out random acts and provoke him to make serious and sometimes fatal mistakes. This was what actually happened. The first reaction was the invasion of Afghanistan and the second was the invasion of Iraq.

The mistakes might happen over and again and there might be other random reactions. Such reactions prompted the Americans and their allies to deal powerful strikes to the head and other important parts of the body of our Ummah, which has been in hibernation for almost two centuries. by Allah's permission, these strikes will help al-ummah to wake from its slumber. Woe unto the Americans, British, and everyone who supports them when our Ummah wakes up.

Our objective, therefore, was to prompt the Americans to come out of their hole and deal powerful strikes to the body of al-Ummah which is in slumber. Without these strikes there would be no hope for this Ummah to wake up. The entire masses of al-Ummah with their financial capabilities and high morale would defeat the enemy. We have a knowledgeable and sincere leadership that has a well examined plan, but we cannot discuss its details at the moment.

The sleeping Ummah will soon wake up. The Americans, their allies, and their minions have been fooled. Abu Mus'ab did not have a previous knowledge of the strike or its goals. After it was accomplished, we explained the objectives to him and briefed him on some important details of the forthcoming goals and expected US reaction. Our assessment was that the strike achieved 20% of what we had planned for. Such an accomplishment was enough to prompt the Americans to carry out the anticipated response.

The Americans were confused in their statements and acts. Their allies and minions were repeating whatever the Americans would say. What we had wished for actually happened. It was crowned by the announcement of junior Bush of his crusade against Islam and Muslims everywhere. The Crusade has been ongoing for a long time. It did not end with the end of the first crusade during the era of Salahuddine and Richard, the heart of the lion.

The Crusade took new dimensions. The ignorance of Bush and his clique in the meaning of this term and its importance to us was a great victory that we extracted from their mouths when they were taken by surprise. Let us go back to Abu Mus'ab, whose stay with us in Kandahar became longer than his stay in Herat.

Abu Mus'ab learned many lessons that played a role inshaping the perspective of the overall conflict in the world between good and evil, the good that is represented by the Messengers and proponents of true messages and evil that is represented by the followers of al-Shaytan and the fabricated and misinterpreted true messages that are based on the wishes of some people in favour of their ambitions and personal interests even though such interest were to the detriment of the poor and deprived among mankind.

The US assault began at the end of 2001. Abu Mus'ab returned to Herat to be close to his brothers and group. We did not have a clear or defined plan for confrontation. There was a significant percentage of Shi'a among the population in the Herat area. The camps and forces of Taliban and their cachets of weapons were fiercely bombarded. The opponents and Shi'a in the region moved swiftly and took control of the area.

The young men of al-Qaeda, Taliban, and Abu Mus'ab's group had no other alternative but to withdraw quickly and join us in eastern Afghanistan. Before Abu Mus'ab and his brothers left Herat, a group of their companions were taken captive by Shi'a forces and opponents. Their release was almost impossible.

Abu Mus'ab, however, reportedly insisted on saving them from captivity. He rallied 25 fighters of his group, performed Salat al-Haja (Prayer of Need), and launched an attack on the area where his companions were taken into custody. The sudden attack took the defending force by surprise. The attack was fierce since it was carried out by a desperate person who did not believe in any solution other than saving his brothers or else die.

The result was the escape of the defending force and the release of all the brothers without casualties. This incident demonstrated the success achieved by Abu Mus'ab over two years. Caring and dedicated men graduated from this camp to defend their principles and companions even if they risked their life. After Abu Mus'ab and his brothers freed their companions, they prepared to leave Herat.

It was a long way to Kandahar. Planes were flying overhead everywhere in Afghanistan. All praise is to Allah, the convoy arrived safely in Kandahar. At the beginning, we decided to defend Kandahar regardless of the consequences. We began to secure the wives and children of the Arab brothers by sending them to Pakistan. We began to make preparations for confrontation.

One day, there was a meeting with some of the important brothers including Abu Mus'ab. One brother used his Thuraya satellite phone. A few minutes after the man used his telephone I left the site of the meeting with three other brothers. Ten minutes after our departure, a US plane shelled the house where we held the meeting. Abu Mus'ab and some brothers were still there.

The bombardment resulted in the collapse of the ceiling of the home. No one was killed but some of the brothers sustained injuries including Abu Mus'ab, who suffered from broken ribs. He had bruises as a result of the collapse of the ceiling.

The assault began on Kandahar. The leadership made a new decision to withdraw to the mountains and evacuate the wounded to safe places. Abu Mus'ab was requested to leave Pakistan since he was wounded. He refused, however, and insisted on joining us to take part in the battle.

The Americans feared direct confrontation. Therefore, they relied on air *bombardment. They employed the hypocrite forces of the Northern Alliance and other opponents in ground battles. Therefore, we can say that Abu Mus'ab did not stay away from the confrontation even though he had a Shar'i excuse to do so.*

The confrontation was not balanced or direct. The objectives of the American assault were centered on the following points:

1. *Overthrow the Islamic Emirate of Afghanistan and eliminate the likelihood of its return or reestablishment any time in the future. The Islamic Emirate provided the circumstances, territory, and safe haven for al-Qaeda. There is no way to allow this to happen again since the reestablishment of this Emirate will lead to the emergence of the Islamic State Khilafa that every Muslim in the world hopes for.*

2. *Annihilate al-Qaeda and its leadership and make it a lesson for everyone. Everyone who dares to harm this giant elephant, the United States, will be punished. Punishment is total extermination. This was one of the major challenges that faced us at the outset of our action. A mature response that would amount to the level of such a challenge was necessary. Thus, the leadership made an audacious decision to dismantle the Emirate and integrate into the Afghan society once again. This move will enable it to the Americans and their supporters of traitors and hypocrites.*

We began to implement the plan immediately. Accordingly, there was no room for us in al- Qaeda to appear in public and continue following the same trends as we did before. It was important to reorganize ourselves once again in all accessible areas in this world.

We Did Not Run Away From the Battle!

Some people might ask: Is this manhood? Are these the principles and values of the faith that you adhere to especially that Islam views the escape from battle as treason?

The answer leans on the following points:

1. We did not run from the battle or leave the brothers of Taliban to face their destiny alone against the Americans. Our plan was to scatter all over and open new and several battlefronts with the Americans to disperse their forces and deny them the chance to focus on one region.

2. The leadership ultimately decided that the form of confrontation was the guerrilla warfare or the hit-and-run tactic. This meant that people who would carry out such warfare should be from the region. Our race and language as Arabs were not suitable for such missions. Those who mastered the languages and dialects of the country had the choice to remain or leave and join other brothers in other areas of conflict.

3. The departure of the brothers and their scattering in other countries provided us with further financial and human resources that we could employ in the battle, particularly that the war was not confined to a specific geographic spot. It was a war everywhere in the world.

4. We realised that these steps were very important for the project to survive. Moreover, they were important to deny the Americans a chance to achieve some of their objectives, including annihilation of the brothers and the leadership.

As a result, all praise is to Allah, we sustained a few casualties, and the leadership was intact and was exercising its work efficiently from Afghanistan. The young men who spread all over the world opened new battlefields with the Americans, polytheists, and hypocrites. The evidence is the outcome that Abu Mus'ab and his brothers achieved in Iraq. I was the man in charge of securing the arrival of some Arab brothers to Iran and relocating them. Abu Mus'ab and his group were among them.

We began to flock to Iran one after the other. The brothers in the Arab Peninsula, Kuwait, and the United Arab Emirates who where outside Afghanistan, had already arrived. They possessed abundant funds. We set up a central leadership circle and subordinate circles. We began to rent apartments for the brothers and some of their families.

The brothers of the Islamic Party of Qalbuddine Hekmatyar offered us satisfactory help in this field. They provided us with apartments and some farms that they owned. They put them at our disposal. We began work and we reestablished contact with the leadership. We began to support it again. This was one of our objectives from leaving Afghanistan. We began to form some groups of fighters to return to Afghanistan to carry out well-prepared missions there. Meanwhile, we began to examine the situation of the group and the brothers to pick newplaces for them.

Abu Mus'ab and his Jordanian and Palestinian comrades opted to go to Iraq, following along debate. Their complexion and accent would enable them to integrate into the Iraqi society easily. Our expectations and profound examination of the situation indicated that the Americans would inevitably make a mistake and invade Iraq sooner or later. Such an invasion would aim at overthrowing the regime. Therefore, we should play an important role in the confrontation and resistance. It would be our historic chance to establish the state of Islam that would play a major role in alleviating injustice and establishing justice in this world, by Allah's permission.

I was in agreement with Abu Mus'ab concerning this analysis. Contrary to what the Americans frequently reiterated, al-Qaeda did not have any relationship with Saddam Hussayn or his regime. The Americans would always try to link Saddam Husayn and his regime to al-Qaeda. They wanted to give themselves justifications and legitimate reasons to enter (Iraq) in harmony with their laws that they dictate by force on this world that is enslaved by the West, the Israelis, and the Anglo-Saxons.

We had to draw up a plan to enter Iraq through the north that was not under the control of the regime. We would then spread south to the areas of our Sunni brothers. The brothers of the Ansar al-Islam Group expressed their willingness to offer assistance to help us achieve this goal.

The Americans felt that Iranians were shutting their eyes to our activity in Iran. Thus, they began to launch a concentrated media campaign against Iran. They accused Iran of helping al-Qaeda and global terrorism. The Iranians responded by pursuing the young men and arresting them. They began to deport them to their former home countries or wherever they wished as long as they left Iran.

Consequently, there was a need for the departure of Abu Mus'ab and the brothers who remained free. The destination was Iraq. The route was the northern border between Iraq and Iran. The goal was to go to Sunni areas in central Iraq and begin to prepare for confrontations to face the US invasion and defeat the Americans, by Allah's permission. The plan was well examined.

Abu Mus'ab gained new experiences. When he saw us off before he left to Iraq, he underlined the importance of taking revenge from the Americans for the crimes they committed during the bombardment of Afghanistan that he witnessed with his own eyes. His hatred and enmity against the Americans shaped his new character. I cannot write in detail about this new personality. I have not met Abu Mus'ab since he left Iran.

The tales I hear about him, however, would allow me to say that he has become a seasoned commander who could run the conflict against the forces of global atheism, the Americans, the Israelis, and their supporters. I hope that Abu Mus'ab and his companions will listen to some of the advice that we believe are important at this stage. Such advice will have great results in determining the outcome of the ongoing conflict between good and evil in the world.